Pretty Funny Tea Cosies

& other beautiful knitted things

To Rhonda,
my beautiful sister

Pretty Funny Tea Cosies

& other beautiful knitted things

LOANI PRIOR

MURDOCH BOOKS

Contents

Yin and Yang

Happy Tea Cosies 6

Technical Stuff

Knitting in the round 8

The stitches and stuff 14

The Projects

Three basic tea cosies 19

Japanese Doll 29

Just an Old-Fashioned Girl 36

Un Joli Petit Cadeau 42

Hawaiian Beauty 48

Hanging Pretty 54

Happy Feet 58

Fruitopia 60

Tutti Frutti Ears 66

She's Apples 74

Heart Throb 80

Hot Potatoes 84

Double Knit Neck Warmer
with Woven Windows 86

Cheroot and Chai 92

Daisy Daisy 98

Tibetan Tea Warriors 102

Ms Daffy Dill 108

Jester Cuppa Tea 114

Russian Caravan 122

Desirée 130

Ranga 138

Froth and Bubble 142

Graphs

Heart Throb 148

Hot Potatoes 152

Double Knit Neck Warmer 154

Abbreviations and terms 157

Stockists 158

Acknowledgements 159

Yin and Yang

Once you can accept the universe as matter
expanding into nothing that is something,
wearing stripes with plaid comes easy.

ALBERT EINSTEIN

Now, you might think that Mr Einstein's assertion has nothing at all to do with tea cosies, but you'd be wrong. It proves that it is perfectly natural, indeed imperative, to temper our large lives with the small and ridiculous things.

Tea cosies provide the yin to our yang.

And so here we are again. Book four!

'I don't feel very much like Pooh today,' said Pooh.
'There, there,' said Piglet. 'I'll bring you tea and honey until you do.'

A.A. MILNE, *WINNIE-THE-POOH*

Happy Tea Cosies

It is only a week from deadline for this knitty manuscript and today, in a serendipitously timely fashion, I received an email from Kimberly. She was afraid her heartfelt words might seem 'a bit weird, "you changed my life" creeperdoodle'. What a WORD. Creeperdoodle! Can I have it, Kimberly? Make it mine? There was nothing creeperdoodle about your letter and I have other beautiful letters like it.

Like Marg's. She wrote, in 2012, saying, 'I discovered you from the *Women's Weekly* article. Am recovering from a broken neck (supposed to be dead but rather be knitting!).' She sent photos of herself with metal scaffolding drilled into her skull and surrounded by all the cosies she'd made.

To those who write to say I have lightened your load, I have not. The truth is, you have found your own strength, your own happy place. Men inhabit their sheds or go fishing for peace of mind, and it is the nature of women to find solace in the gentle arts, on our own and alongside others, and to while away the darkness of our ill health or sadness, with our click-clacking. It is a surprisingly common story.

Well, alright, OK – I LOVE that you do it in the company of my funny cosies.

I love that you love my cosies. All of you. And that you tell me. I love that too. Oh, it is just a big old tea cosy love-in, that's what it is. You make me feel very much like Pooh.

Technical Stuff

'Really, all you need to become a good knitter are wool, needles, hands, and slightly below-average intelligence. Of course superior intelligence, such as yours and mine, is an advantage.'

ELIZABETH ZIMMERMANN, *KNITTING WITHOUT TEARS*

Ain't got noth'n' to add to that.

- -

Knitting in the round

One discovered knitting in the round quite late in life and has worried over most methods, BUT there is a favourite, after all, and it has to be the Magic Loop. That is not to say that there isn't a place for using double-pointed needles or two sets of circular needles, but that is for you to sort out for yourself. They are all described beautifully in One's previous tea cosy books and there is always that knitting gold mine, YouTube. What DID we do before the worldwide web?

The Magic Loop
(one set of circular needles)

EQUIPMENT

One set of circular needles with a long cable length –
80 cm (32 in) from needle tip to needle tip will do the
job nicely for a tea cosy knitted in the round using the
Magic Loop.

METHOD 1

Casting on and joining the cast-on stitches

Cast on the required number of stitches, plus one. If
the pattern says cast on 40 stitches, you'll cast on 41.
Halve the stitches (with the extra stitch on the side of
the working yarn) and pull the cable out into a loop
between the two centre stitches (Pic 1).

Slide all the stitches up onto the needles. Check that
your cast-on stitches are not twisted. Place the last
cast-on stitch onto the needle holding the first cast-on
stitch (Pic 2), slide the bottom stitches down onto the
flexible cable and then knit the first cast-on and the last
cast-on stitches together. You are joined!

Pic 1

extra stitch

Pic 2

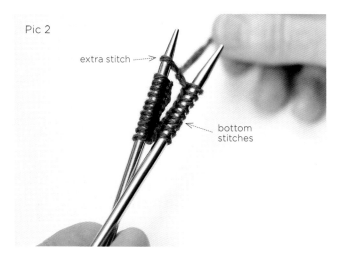

extra stitch

bottom
stitches

METHOD 2

The holy cast-on

Because there is no hole!
And because it is heavenly.

This method is used only when you start with a small number of stitches and you want a closed hole in the middle of a circle. You need one set of circular needles.

One has never seen this method of casting on in the round before, but that doesn't mean One was first to invent it. But if One was, then One is very pleased with oneself.

Step 1 Make a circle of yarn around the first two fingers on your left hand. Place one needle in your right hand. Let the other needle dangle down. You don't need it yet. The needle in your right hand is your working needle.

Step 2 Insert your working needle into the loop, front to back and wrap the needle with your working yarn. Bring the working needle through to the front of the loop so that you now have a little loop sitting on your needle. It is still just a loop and not yet a stitch.

Step 3 To make the stitch, bring the yarn forward of the needle, pick up the little loop sitting on the needle with your left hand and bring it over the top of the yarn and off the needle.

Step 1

Step 2

Step 3

Step 4 Draw down on the working yarn to tighten the stitch. Repeat the process until you have the required number of stitches.

Step 5 Move the stitches down onto the flexible cable of the circular needles. Halve the stitches and draw the flexible cable out into a loop at this halfway mark.

Step 6 Find the short tail of the yarn and gently pull on it to draw the stitches into a closed circle.

You are ready to start knitting in the round with the Magic Loop method.

Step 4

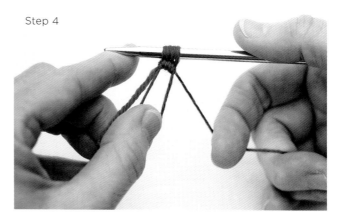

Step 5

Step 6

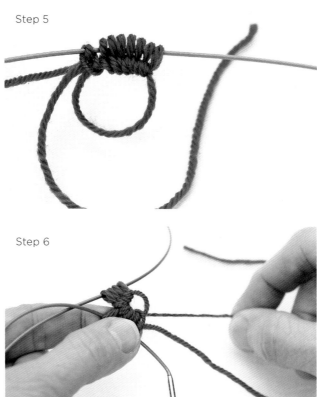

Knitting in the round with the Magic Loop

Knit half the round, then set up the needles and cables ready to knit the other half round. You need one needlepoint to knit from (holding the stitches) and one needlepoint to knit with (free of stitches) - see below.

Very important note. You will NEVER have the wrong side facing you when you are knitting in the round. Remember you are NOT working back and forth in ROWS, you are working round and round in ROUNDS. Dizzy yet?

Always keep the cable looped at each halfway mark.

When you start a tea cosy from the top down, knitting in the round, and then come to the Sides, which are to be worked in ROWS, leave half the stitches in the centre of the cable and ignore them while you work down the OTHER side with the needlepoints.

Note. Avoiding extra stitches. The most common mistake when knitting in the round is to add a stitch at the change-over of needles, in all methods. Take your time to arrange the working thread so that it is not wrapped around needles or cables.

METHOD 3
Joining two sides of a cosy

If you already have two separate Sides of a tea cosy that you want to join in the round, un-knit the last stitch just before the point of join. Increase into the last stitch by knitting into the front and back of it.

Place the last (increased) stitch on the needle holding the waiting stitches (see below), reset your needles ready to knit the second half and knit two together

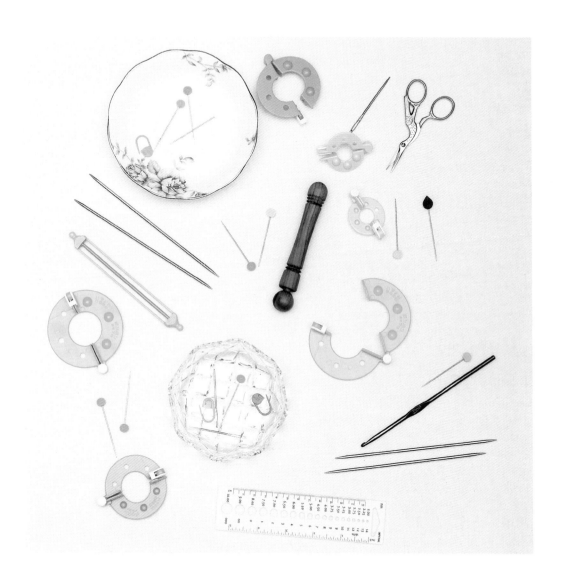

The stitches and stuff

I always say, I do, I always say, knitting is easy. If you know how to knit a stitch, purl a stitch, cast on and off, you can do anything. Well, here are a few 'anythings' you will need in this book.

Loop stitch

Pic 1

You will be knitting into the front and back of the next stitch and making a loop by wrapping it around your thumb at the front of the work.

Place the working needle into the next stitch, knitwise. Bring the yarn forward through the middle of the two needles and wrap it around your left thumb at the front of the work and then back through the two needles, the way it came (Pic 1).

Place the working needle into the back of the same stitch and knit it off the (left) holding needle. Now you have two stitches on your (right) working needle instead of one.

Pic 2

Place your left needle into the front of the two stitches (with the loop in the middle) and knit them together (Pic 2).

Take the time to tighten it into a bit of a knot. Yes! Every stitch! It will be worth it.

Increase once in next stitch

This is a way of increasing by knitting into the front and back of the next stitch.

M1 – make 1

This is different from 'increase once in next stitch'. To Make 1 (M1) is to increase by lifting up the connecting thread between the stitch you have just worked and the stitch you are about to work, onto the left (waiting) needle. The left (waiting) needle should lift the connecting thread from front to back. Place your right (working) needle into the back of the loop (new stitch) and knit.

SSK – slip, slip, knit

This is a way of decreasing to make the stitches lean towards the left when the knitted fabric is facing you. Slip one stitch knitwise, slip another stitch knitwise. Insert the left needle into the front of the two slipped stitches and knit them together through the back.

K2Tog – knit 2 together

This is a way of decreasing to make the stitches lean towards the right when the knitted fabric is facing you. Place your working needle into the next two stitches knitwise and knit them together.

I-cord

You need 2 x 4 mm (UK 8, USA 6) double-pointed needles.

Cast on 4 stitches.

Do not turn your work. Slide the 4 stitches up to the other end of the double-pointed needle, draw the yarn across the back of the work and knit 4 stitches.

Repeat over and over until you have the required length.

Cut off a long thread and, with a darning needle, draw closed the remaining 4 stitches. Sew a couple of stitches to hold in place.

Mattress stitch

Mattress stitch is a beaut way to sew up two pieces of knitted fabric. The stitches are hidden and the seam is seamless. Lay the two edges side by side, with the right sides facing you. Thread a darning needle with yarn that matches the edges you are joining. Working from bottom to top, pick up the first stitch (adjacent to the cast-off) on the right-hand edge, and then pick up the first stitch (adjacent to the cast-off) on the left-hand edge. Continue working right edge, left edge, four or five times, and then pull the thread tight, drawing the edges together. The seam will magically disappear. Continue to the end of the seam in this manner.

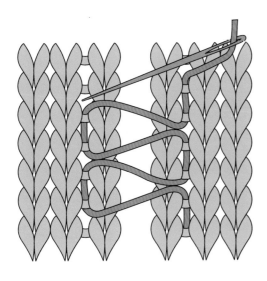

Wonder weave

Wonder weave is a very clever but simple way to make a completely different sort of fabric. It is just garter stitch fabric, woven later with a darning needle and thread. For best effect, use three contrasting colours. The sample is in Pink, Green and Blue.

It can be done with any size yarn and needles.

The knitting

Cast on the number of stitches the pattern requires. (I cast on in Pink.)

Knit one row (Pink).

Add in the second colour (Green) and knit 2 rows.

Add in the third colour (Blue) and knit 2 rows.

Return to the first colour (Pink) and knit 2 rows.

And that's all the knitting part is. Two rows Pink, 2 rows Green, 2 rows Cream, over and over.

In the diagram (opposite), the work has been turned so that the cast-on edge is at the top – but it doesn't matter which edge you start from.

The weaving

Think of the garter stitches as being lined up in columns – a column of ∪ loops and right up beside it, hugging it – a column of ∩ loops. There are only TWO kinds of columns BUT there are THREE colours.

With a darning needle and the Pink yarn, begin with a ∪ column – weave UNDER, over, under, over, and so on.

Miss 2 columns.

Then, on an ∩ column – with the same Pink yarn – weave the opposite: OVER, under, over, under, and so on.

Miss 2 columns, then on a ∪ column, weave UNDER, over, under, over, and so on. Repeat until you have finished all the Pink columns. Check very carefully as you set up this first colour (Pink). Get this right and the rest will be easy. Now go back and fill in the gaps with the Green yarn, then the Blue yarn.

Cut only a workable length of yarn for weaving. When that length is close to the end, take it to the back of the work. Cut a new length of yarn and start the weaving where you left off, drawing the needle up from the back of the fabric. The end and the beginning yarns can be tied off on the wrong side later.

The resulting fabric does not have the same top to bottom stretch that normal knitted fabric has, but damn, it looks fabulous!

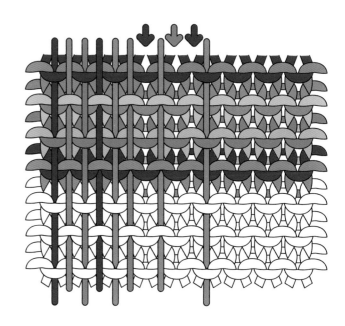

No2: Curvy rib cosy

- -

METHOD
Knitted in the round from the top down.

Body
Upper body
Work the Upper Body as for the Basic Tea Cosy No 1, until you reach the Sides.

Sides
Up to this point, you have been working round and round. Now you are going to work BACK and FORTH in ROWS. Find the point where the working yarn is. This becomes the first stitch of the first ROW on one SIDE of the cosy.

Begin working the first Side with the wrong side facing.

Note. Now that you have come to the Sides, which are to be worked in ROWS, leave half the stitches in the centre of the cable and ignore them while you work down the OTHER side with the needlepoints.

Row 1: K1, P1, place marker (pm). Purl to the last 2 stitches, K1, P1.

Row 2: (K1, P1) twice, K1, pm, knit to 1 stitch before marker, P1, remove marker (rm), K1, P1.

Row 3: (K1, P1) three times, pm, purl to 1 stitch before marker, K1, rm, (P1, K1) twice, P1.

Row 4: (K1, P1) four times, K1, pm, knit to 1 stitch before marker, P1, rm, rib to end of row.

Row 5: (K1, P1) five times, pm, purl to 1 stitch before marker, K1, rm, rib to end of row.

See how you are creating a ribbed pattern, row by row, in from the edges of the tea cosy sides. It forms a lovely curve getting from stocking stitch to ribbed stitch and makes a simple base just that much more classy.

Row 6: (K1, P1) six times, K1, pm, knit to 1 stitch before marker, P1, rm, rib to end of row.

Row 7: (K1, P1) seven times, pm, purl to 1 stitch before marker, K1, rm, rib to end of row.

Row 8: (K1, P1) eight times, K1, pm, knit to 1 stitch before marker, P1, rm, rib to end of row.

If you started with 72 stitches in the round, 36 stitches on each side, then you will now be up to rib stitch all the way across.

Row 9: Rib to end of row.

(If you started with more stitches, continue adding an extra rib on the inside edges of the curve on every row, until you can rib all the way across.)

Continue in rib stitch down Side One of the cosy base until it measures all the way to the table. So that means you need to try it on your pot.

Repeat the same instructions for the second Side. Remember you started with the WRONG SIDE of the tea cosy facing.

Putting it all together

Sew the Sides together below the spout and handle using mattress stitch (see page 16).

No3: Picot edge cosy

- -

METHOD
The Body and the lining are knitted all in one piece, which features a very pretty picot edge hem to join the two.

Body
Upper body and sides
Work Upper Body and Sides as for the Basic Tea Cosy No 1 (working the Sides in stocking stitch, if you like, rather than a rib), BUT instead of completing the Sides, work both Sides to measure just below the spout and handle of the teapot. Do not cast off.

Picot edge hem
Join in the round again, using Method 3 (see page 12).

Work 5 rounds stocking stitch (OR until the cosy Body is long enough to cover the whole teapot).

Rnd 6: *Yfwd, K2tog, repeat from * to end of round.
Rnd 7: Knit every stitch.

Note. The yfwd becomes one large stitch and, as you knit into it, a lace hole forms.

Work 5 rounds stocking stitch (OR the same number of rounds you made on the way into the picot edge).

This is the end of the Picot Edge Hem.

Continuing the lining
You might like to cast off right here and sew the hem up into place, but I'm going to keep going to make the Lining.

Divide the stitches into two again and knit up one Side – one row shorter than you knitted on the way down. Repeat on the other Side of the cosy.

Join in the round again, using Method 3. Gees, you'll be good at this by now.

It is time to DECREASE in the round to form the top inside of the lining and you need to exercise a little maths.

Divide everything by 8.

If you have 80 stitches in the round, then you have 8 segments of 10 stitches each. If you have 72 stitches in the round, then you have 8 segments of 9 stitches each. 64 stitches in the round, divided by 8 segments, is 8 stitches. Etc. I knew there was a reason to learn my times tables at school.

To decrease from 80 stitches:
Rnd 1: *K8, K2tog, repeat from * to end of round.
Rnd 2 (and each alternate round): Knit.
Rnd 3: *K7, K2tog, repeat from * to end of round.
Rnd 5: *K6, K2tog, repeat from * to end of round.
Rnd 7: *K5, K2tog, repeat from * to end of round.

You get the picture.

When there are 16 stitches left, decrease one more time WITHOUT the alternate 'Knit' round. There are 8 stitches left and the lining is slightly smaller than the outer. Cut the yarn leaving a long piece to thread through the remaining stitches with a darning needle and draw up tight. Make a couple of holding stitches.

Fussing over it a bit and then putting it all together

Fold the smaller lining up inside the Body. Sew the lining to the Body around the spout and handle.

Heirlooms

A tea cosy makes a fabulous handmade gift. It is quirky, practical and no one has to wear it. It will very soon be coveted. 'Mum, err, I was wondering, when you pop off to the great tea party in the sky, you know, in a really long time, when you are extremely old and ready to depart this mortal coil, can I please have your tea cosy?' Or more directly, 'I'm having that tea cosy when you die.'

But these particular quirky, practical handmade things are also delicate, graceful, pretty, pretty things. Can you not imagine them as the most beautiful gift on the occasion of an important birthday, or a wedding, or just for the love of a sister, a daughter, or your mum, whose tea cosy you are about to covet right back?

To make these delicate things you need delicate wool. Me and Zauberball, we are like young lovers and when I'm not with my old flame, Noro, I want to be with Ms Z all the time. They are very different from each other, Zauberball and Noro, but they both come in the most glorious colours. Don't be fooled by the large numbers on Ms Z's price tag. There is a lot of yardage in one 100 g (3½ oz) ball. The next few pages are filled to the brim with Colour 2079, Flower Garden.

Japanese Doll

Petite, delicate, but oh, so operatic.

FOR AKARI

SIZE

To fit a two-cup teapot that stands 9 cm (3½ in) tall (not including the knob) and 10 cm (4 in) in diameter (not including the spout and handle).

MATERIALS

1 x 100 g (3½ oz) ball Schoppel Wolle Zauberball sock yarn: Colour 2079 (Flower Garden) (see Note)

EQUIPMENT

* One set 3 mm (UK 11, USA 2/3) circular needles, 80 cm (32 in) from tip to tip – Cosy
* One pair 3 mm (UK 11, USA 2/3) double-pointed needles – Sash
* Darning needle
* Stitch holder

METHOD

Body is knitted in the round from the bottom up.

Note. As for Just an Old-Fashioned Girl (see page 36), you need to wind the wool into its three colours, Pink, Green and Cream. The pattern begins the same way as for the old girl, same wool, same number of stitches, but I have used smaller needles. OK, I admit. It wasn't intentional. I didn't read my own pattern properly. So, smaller needles, smaller cosy. And you guessed it, if you used an 8-ply (DK) yarn and 4 mm (UK 8, USA 6) needles, you'd get a bigger cosy.

Cosy

Body

With 3 mm (UK 11, USA 2/3) circular needles and Cream yarn, cast on 100 (+ 1) stitches and join in the round using Method 1 (see page 9).

Rnds 1–7: Knit.

Picot edge hem and sides

Continue the pattern as for Just an Old-Fashioned Girl (see page 36), until the bottom Picot Edge Hem and the two Sides of the cosy are complete. Then come back here.

In the round again

When the two Sides are the same length (measure in row numbers, not in centimetres/inches) and you are ready for a knit row (right side facing) – join in the round again. Don't use any of the methods described in the techniques pages; just knit straight across from one side to the other, pulling the travelling yarns tight across the back. This will continue the pink and green stripes up in a nice line above the spout and handle openings. A couple of stitches with a darning needle and thread will secure the join later.

Note about adding in new yarn. The colour changes shade as you knit, light to dark to light again. When you add in a new ball, you might have to wind it to the point where it matches the shades of Pink or Green to the fabric already knitted.

Rnd 1: *(K2, P3, K2) (Pink), (K2, P3, K2) (Green), repeat from * to end of round.

Rnd 2: *(K2tog, K3, ssk) (Pink), (K2tog, K3, ssk) (Green), repeat from * to end of round (100 sts).

Rnds 3 & 4: *K5 (Pink), K5 (Green), repeat from * to end of round.

Rnd 5: *(K2, P3, K2) (Pink), (K2, P3, K2) (Green), repeat from * to end of round.

Rnds 6 & 7: *K5 (Pink), K5 (Green), repeat from * to end of round.

Rnd 8: *(K2tog, P1, ssk) (Pink), (K2tog, P1, ssk) (Green), repeat from * to end of round (60 sts).

Rnds 9 & 10: *K3 (Pink), K3 (Green), repeat from * to end of round.

Rnd 11: Using both the Pink and Green yarns together, *K2tog, repeat from * to end of round (30 sts).

Rnd 12: Using both yarns together, knit.

Rnd 13: Using both yarns together, *K2tog, repeat from * to end of round (15 sts).

Rather than casting off, cut the yarn 20 cm (8 in) from the knitting and thread a darning needle with it. Draw the thread up through the remaining 15 stitches but don't draw into a tight circle. You want to make a straight seam sitting up in a ridge to sit the Bodice on, as shown in the photo (opposite). Be sure to line the ridge up with the spout and handle openings.

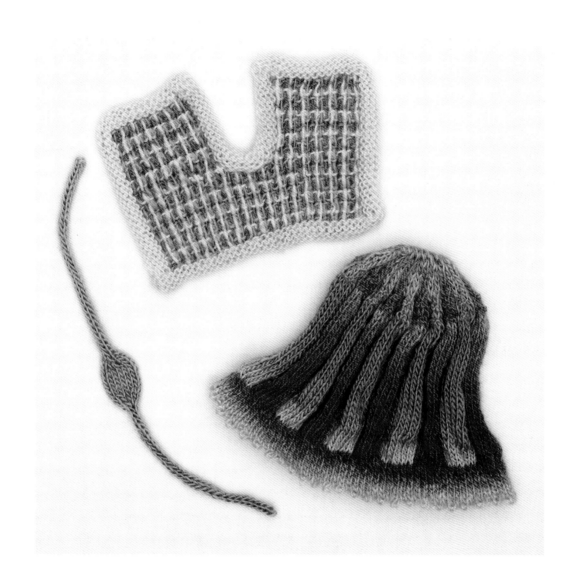

Bodice

The Bodice is knitted in rows, in garter stitch first, and then with needle and yarn woven into this beautiful piece of fabric. The Rolled Edge comes last.

Bodice back

With 3 mm (UK 11, USA 2/3) circular needles and Pink yarn, cast on 28 stitches. Knit 1 row. Join in the Green yarn and knit 2 rows. Join in the Cream yarn and knit 2 rows. Bring the Pink yarn up and knit 2 rows. Bring the Green yarn up and knit 2 rows. Continue in this fashion until you count 12 rows (including the cast-on row). You should end on a (2nd) Cream row.

Note. The edge with the yarns travelling up the side will be a little messy. Do your best to tighten the last stitch of each row as you begin the next – but don't fret too much – it will all be covered later on by the Rolled Edges.

Bodice front

To set up for the front, work the next 12 stitches (Right Front Bodice) in Pink. Place the middle 4 stitches on a piece of yarn to hold the stitches to return to later, as part of the Rolled Edge. Place the last 12 stitches (Left Front Bodice) on a stitch holder.

Return to the Right Front Bodice, continue in pattern until 12 rows are completed and then cast off.

Place the stitches from the Left Front Bodice back onto the needles and continue in pattern as for the Right Front Bodice. Cast off.

Weaving

Think of the fabric as having ROWS and COLUMNS. You have already produced the ROWS of Pink, Green and Cream. Now, with a needle and yarn, you are going to weave in the COLUMNS of Pink, Green and Cream. Get over to page 16, see how it's done and do it.

Rolled edge

Start with the front and neck opening. The circular needles come into their own here. With the right side facing, using 3 mm (UK 11, USA 2/3) circular needles and Cream yarn, pick up 12 or 13 stitches along the Right Front Bodice opening. Knit the 4 stitches from the neck back. Pick up 12 or 13 stitches along the Left Front Bodice opening.

Row 1: Knit.
Row 2: Purl.

Repeat these 2 rows twice more (6 rows in total).

Cast off.

Do not sew any of the Rolled Edges under until you have completed all of them.

Refer to the Rolled Edge diagram (opposite).

Rolled Edge diagram

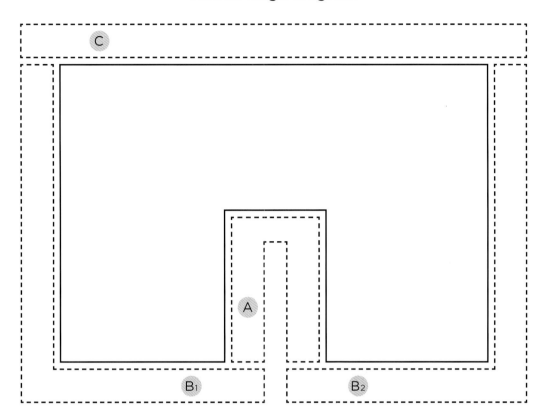

You have just completed A. With the right side facing, pick up stitches for B1. I'm not going to give you a number of stitches. You'll know what to do. Pick up around the corner (you might like to put a loop in your circular needles at this point) and across the Right Front of the Bodice. When you arrive at Rolled Edge A, continue to pick up stitches across the 6 rows you made there. Work the rolled edge B1 from Row 1, as you did for A, but with a little addition. When you get to the bendy corner on a knit row, make 1 stitch (see page 15). Do that for each of the knit rows.

That's enough instruction. Off you go and do B2 and C. Now all you have to do is hem the Rolled Edge neatly under.

Sash

With 3 mm (UK 11, USA 2/3) double-pointed needles and Green yarn, cast on 4 stitches. Work i-cord (see page 15) for 10 cm (4 in). To work the sash waist, turn the work as you would in normal row knitting so that you have the wrong side facing.

Row 1: Purl.
Row 2: (K1, M1) 3 times, K1 (7 sts).
Row 3: Purl.
Row 4: K3, M1, K1, M1, K3 (9 sts).
Row 5: Purl.
Row 6: Knit.

Row 7: Purl.
Repeat the last 2 rows once more.
Row 10: K2, ssk, K1, K2tog, K2 (7 sts).
Row 11: Purl.
Row 12: Ssk, ssk, K2tog, K1 (4 sts).
Work i-cord for another 10 cm (4 in) and tie off. Remember, you will not turn the work, but slip the stitches up to the other end of the double-pointed needles and bring the yarn across the back to knit the first stitch.

Lining

No need for a Lining. She is already warm and sturdy.

Putting it all together

Fold and pin the bottom picot edge hem up and sew into place, taking care to line up the lace holes to form the picot edge.

Secure the back of the Bodice to the back side of the rim on top of the cosy with a few light stitches. Secure the front of the Bodice to the front side of the rim on top of the cosy. Wrap the green Sash around the waist, crossing over the i-cords at the back before bringing them to the front again for a simple tie. Secure it all into place with a few hidden stitches.

Cosy

Lower body

With 3.5 mm (UK 9/10, USA 4) circular needles and Creamy White or Palest Pink Zauberball yarn, cast on 100 (+ 1) stitches and join in the round using Method 1 (see page 9).

Rnds 1–7: Knit.

𝒩ote. This particular Zauberball yarn is beautifully and cleverly dyed three colours. Before you do anything else, you need to wind the wool into two balls, one ball starting with Pink and the other ball starting with Green. It might take a bit more balling and cutting and sorting than just halving it and it isn't absoLUTEly necessary to organise the colours like a control freak ... but I did.

Picot edge hem

Rnd 8: *Yfwd, K2tog, repeat from * to end of round.
Rnd 9: Knit every stitch (still 100 sts – 50 sts on each side).

𝒩ote. The yfwd becomes one large stitch and, as you knit into it, a lace hole forms.

Rnds 10–15: Knit.
Rnd 16: *K2, M1, K3, M1, repeat from * to end of round (140 sts: 70 sts on each side of your Magic Loop).
Rnd 17: Join in the other colour (Green). *K7 (Pink), K7 (Green), repeat from * to end of round, pulling the travelling yarn tightly across the back of the work so that the stitches are all scrunched together on the needle. This forms the pleated fabric.
Rnds 18–22: As for Rnd 17.

Side one

Time to knit in ROWS and not rounds, up each Side of the cosy. Put half the stitches to sleep. Ignore them.

Turn the work so that the WRONG side is facing you and the working yarn is coming from the first stitch on the needle.

Row 1: *P7 (Green), P7 (Pink), repeat from * to end of row. (Again, pull the travelling yarn tightly across the front (wrong side) of the work to form the pleated fabric.)
Row 2: *K7 (Pink), K7 (Green), repeat from * to end of row.

𝒯ip. It is essential to twist the two yarns around each other at the beginning of every row before making the first stitch.

Repeat these 2 rows until Side One reaches just above the spout and handle of the teapot.

Cut and tie off the two yarns. Put these stitches to sleep and return to the other side.

Side two

With the WRONG side facing, join in the Green and, when you come to it, the Pink. Repeat Rows 1 and 2, as for Side One.

Upper body

When the two Sides are the same length (measure in row numbers not in centimetres/inches) and you are ready for a knit row (right side facing) – join in the ROUND again. Don't use any of the methods described in the techniques pages! Just knit straight across from one side to the other, pulling the travelling yarns tightly across the back.

Continue knitting in pattern for another 2–3 cm (¾–1¼ in). When you think the cosy is sitting up high enough above the teapot, cut the Pink and Green yarn and choose a Creamy White/Palest Pink to continue in for the Top Picot Edge Band.

Top picot edge band

Rnd 1: Knit.
Rnd 2: *K1, K2tog, K2, K2tog, repeat from * to end round (100 sts).
Rnds 3–8: Knit.
Rnd 9: *Yfwd, K2tog, repeat from * to end of round (to form the picot edge).
Rnd 10: Knit every stitch to complete picot edge.
Rnds 11–16: Knit.
Rnds 17–22: *K1, P1, repeat from * to end of round.
Rnd 23: *K2tog, repeat from * to end of round (50 sts).
Rnd 24: Knit.
Rnd 25: *K3, K2tog, repeat from * to end of round (40 sts).

Rnd 26: Knit.
Rnd 27: *K2, K2tog, repeat from * to end of round (30 sts).
Rnd 28: Knit.
Rnd 29: *K1, K2tog, repeat from * to end of round (20 sts).
Rnd 30: Knit.
Rnd 31: *K2tog, repeat from * to end of round (10 sts).

Cut the yarn leaving a long tail. Use a darning needle to thread the end of the yarn through the remaining stitches and draw up tight. Make a couple of stitches to secure the centre.

Lining

I don't reckon there is a need for a Lining in this little beauty. She is warm and sturdy enough already, with all those folds.

Bell flower – make lots
Bell

With 3 mm (UK 11, USA 2/3) circular needles and the pink hues of Zauberball yarn, refer to Method 2, The Holy Cast-On (see page 10) to cast on 6 stitches.

Rnd 1: Knit. Place marker to show the beginning of the round.
Rnd 2: Increase once in every stitch (by knitting into the front and back of it) to end of round (12 sts).
Rnd 3: Knit.
Rnd 4: *K3, M1, repeat from * to end of round (16 sts).
Rnds 5–10: Knit.
Rnd 11: *K4, M1, repeat from * to end of round (20 sts).
Rnd 12: Knit.
Rnd 13: K2, *M1, K5, repeat from * to last 3 sts, M1, K3 (24 sts).
Rnds 14 & 15: Knit.

Rnd 16: *Yfwd, K2tog, repeat from * to end of round (to form the picot edge).

Rnds 17 & 18: Knit.

Rnd 19: *K4, K2tog, repeat from * to end of round (20 sts).

Rnd 20: Knit.

Rnd 21: K1, K2tog, *K3, K2tog, repeat from * to last 2 sts, K2 (16 sts).

Rnds 22–26: Knit.

Rnd 27: *K2, K2tog, repeat from * to end of round (12 sts).

Rnd 28: Knit.

Rnd 29: *K2tog, repeat from * to end of round (6 sts).

Instead of casting off, thread the end through a darning needle and through the last 6 stitches. Pull up tight to close the hole and sew a couple of holding stitches. Fold the Bell in on itself, along the picot edging, with the larger section down inside the smaller section. Pull through the remaining wool to use later when attaching the flowers.

Leaf

With 3 mm (UK 11, USA 2/3) circular needles and the green hues of Zauberball yarn, refer to Method 2, The Holy Cast-On (see page 10) to cast on 8 stitches.

Rnd 1: (K3, P1) twice.

Rnd 2: (K1, M1, K1, M1, K1, P1) twice (12 sts).

Rnd 3: (K5, P1) twice.

Rnd 4: (K2, M1, K1, M1, K2, P1) twice (16 sts).

Rnd 5: (K7, P1) twice.

Rnd 6: (K3, M1, K1, M1, K3, P1) twice (20 sts).

Rnds 7-9: (K9, P1) twice.

Rnd 10: (K2, ssk, K1, K2tog, K2, P1) twice (16 sts).

Rnds 11-13: (K7, P1) twice.

Rnd 14: (K1, ssk, K1, K2tog, K1, P1) twice (12 sts).

Rnds 15 & 16: (K5, P1) twice.

Rnd 17: (Ssk, K1, K2tog, P1) twice (8 sts).

Rnd 18: (K3, P1) twice.

Rnd 19: (Ssk, K1, slip back stitch over front stitch on working needle, P1) twice (4 sts).

Cut a long length of wool and thread a darning needle. Thread the end yarn through the last 4 stitches carefully and use your cleverest, neatest sewing skills to make the pointiest Leaf tip.

The underlined K1 forms the centre vein of the Leaf. Line the veins up on either side of the Leaf and, with your needle and thread, sew the back and front together down the vein.

Putting it all together

Fold and pin the bottom hem up and sew into place, taking care to line up the lace holes to form the picot edge.

Place the cosy on the pot and let your 'flower arranger' loose. If your Leaves and Bell Flowers aren't spilling over, make more! Arrange everything before you sew anything. Remove everything except the two bottom Leaves. Stitch into place. Arrange everything again. Remove everything but two bottom Flowers. Stitch into place. Arrange everything again. You get the picture.

I quite like the little lean to the front left of my Old-Fashioned Girl. It is just a tiny bit cheeky. A tiny bit naughty. Not all sugar and spice.

Un Joli Petit Cadeau

A little something to carry something a little shiny in?

MATERIALS

* I used my leftover Zauberball and Zauberball 100 yarn in various colours

EQUIPMENT

* One set 3 mm (UK 11, USA 2/3) circular needles, 80 cm (32 in) from tip to tip
* One pair 3 mm (UK 11, USA 2/3) double-pointed needles
* Darning needle
* Scissors

Gift bag

Note. The pattern starts at the bottom of the bag and uses the double knitting method to knit the front and back of the bag at the same time – backwards and forwards in rows. This method gives a nice stretchy seam along the bottom of the bag. It also provides an opportunity to understand what double knitting is and how it works.

Lower bag
Begun with double knitting.

With 3 mm (UK 11, USA 2/3) circular needles and Zauberball, cast on 36 stitches. (Yes, you are working in ROWS but use the circular needles. You need them to work in ROUNDS later on.)

Another note. It is essential that you pay attention to the placement of your yarn while double knitting. All will become clear.

Row 1 (front): *Yarn back, K1, yfwd, slip 1 purlwise, repeat from * to end of row.
Row 2 (back): *Yarn back, K1, yfwd, slip 1 purlwise, repeat from * to end of row.
Repeat Rows 1 and 2 five more times (12 rows in all).

Final note. If you accidentally purl the stitch instead of only SLIPPING it purlwise, you will join the front and back fabrics together. A big no no.

Tip about neat edging. Just before you get to the end of the row, with about three stitches to go, bring the stitches on both the left and right needles right up to the tip. Work the last stitches small and close to the tips so that you don't stretch that last stitch. Turn and work the first stitches close to the tip and then continue on as you would again – until the last three stitches.

Upper bag
Continued with knitting in the round with the Magic Loop.

Setting up
To separate the front and back fabrics of the double knitting, hold 2 double-pointed needles (dpns) in one hand as a pair and slip the stitches from the circular needles onto the dpns, a stitch from the front onto the front dpn, a stitch from the back onto the back dpn, back and forth to the end of the row. You should now have all the stitches from the back fabric on one dpn and all the stitches from the front fabric on the other dpn.

But! We don't want to knit on dpns. We want to knit in the round with the circular needles, now the front and back fabric are separated. Beginning at the point where the working thread hangs, slip the stitches back onto the circular needles, one side at a time. Leave a loop in the cable at the end of the first 18 stitches and, working in the round, slip the next 18 stitches.

Mark the beginning of the round with a contrasting colour thread.

Rnd 7: Knit.

𝓝ote. Round SEVEN? I hear you ask. Yes. You worked 12 ROWS but you made 6 ROUNDS.

Rnd 8: K5, P8, knit to end of round.
Repeat the last round 11 more times (12 rounds in all).
Rnds 20–25: Knit.
Make the lace holes as follows:
Rnd 26: *Yfwd, K2tog, repeat from * to end of round.
Rnds 27–30: Knit.

The little gift bags that match Hawaiian Beauty (see page 49) are cast off at this point. The little gift bags that match Japanese Doll (see page 29) are continued to make the pretty picot edge like this ...

Rnd 31: *Yfwd, K2tog, repeat from * to end of round.
Rnds 32 & 33: Knit.

Cast off and fold the last two rows down inside to form the picot edge at the top of the little gift bag and with needle and yarn, hem.

Weaving

The weaving described on page 16 is done on garter stitch. You have made a little window of the wrong side of stocking stitch, but the principle is exactly the same. The most important thing is to take your time and make sure that all the stitches in each column in the reverse stocking stitch square are lined up.

Drawstring

With 3 mm (UK 11, USA 2/3) dpns and Zauberball yarn, cast on 3 stitches and make a length of i-cord (see page 15), about 26 cm (10 in) long. Thread the i-cord drawstring through the lace holes in the gift bag.

Girly Gifts

More than twenty years ago, a girlfriend gave me three hangers, padded and covered in pretty white broderie anglaise. I hang my best blouses on them still and I am reminded of Linda. You could take up residence in someone's wardrobe and knit them a coat hanger cover.

Or a pair of no-shoes ... you know ... for the girl who has everything, even a tea cosy or three. Bet she doesn't own no-shoes. When One was a gel (spoken with a hard 'g' and a posh accent), One made no-shoes, out of raffia paper and a daisy maker, for sale, to save up money to buy a violin. One did buy a violin. Perhaps One ought to have simply stuck to making no-shoes after all.

Hawaiian Beauty

Ta Da! The Zauberball again. Colour 1701: Parrot, with a hint of 1564: Tropical Fish in the frangipani flowers. Not necessary to buy a whole ball of wool for a splash of something different. But I couldn't resist. And besides, I'm in line to win that prize of all prizes, dying with the most yarn.

FOR JULIE OF CARBROOK, WOT KNITTED ALL THOSE FLOWERS

SIZE

To fit a four-cup teapot that stands 11 cm (4¼ in) tall (not including the knob) and 14 cm (5½ in) in diameter (not including the spout and handle).

MATERIALS

* 1 x 100 g (3½ oz) ball Schoppel Wolle Zauberball 100 yarn: Colour 1701 (Parrot) – Outer Cosy, Pillbox Hat and Frangipani Flowers (see Note)
* 1 x 50 g (1¾ oz) ball sturdy 4-ply yarn – Lining
* 30 cm (12 in) square stiff interfacing

EQUIPMENT

* One set 3 mm (UK 11, USA 2/3) circular needles, 80 cm (32 in) from tip to tip
* Stitch holder (or another set of circular needles)
* Darning needle
* Scissors

METHOD

Knitted in the round from the top down.

Note. Ball all the apricot tones of the Zauberball yarn out separately from the rest of the yarn. Use the apricot colours for the Frangipani Flowers and all the other colours for the Outer Cosy and Pillbox Hat.

Outer cosy/lining

Upper body

With 3 mm (UK 11, USA 2/3) circular needles and Zauberball 100, refer to Method 2, The Holy Cast-On (see page 10) to cast on 8 stitches.

Rnd 1 (and each alternate round): Knit.
Rnd 2: Increase once in every stitch (by knitting into the front and back of it) to end of round (16 sts).
Rnd 4: *K1, increase once in next stitch, repeat from * to end of round (24 sts).
Rnd 6: *K2, increase once in next stitch, repeat from * to end of round (32 sts).
Rnd 8: *K3, increase once in next stitch, repeat from * to end of round (40 sts).
Rnd 10: *K4, increase once in next stitch, repeat from * to end of round (48 sts).

Continue in this increasing pattern until there are 10 stitches in each segment of the pie (80 sts in total). Measure against your teapot. You may need to keep increasing. Measure again.

Knit one more round.

Sides

Up to this point you have been working round and round. Now, you are going to work BACK and FORTH in ROWS. Because you are now working in ROWS, and working back across the stitches you have just made (not onto the next stitch in the round), you will have the reverse side of the knitting facing you. Find the point where the working yarn is. This becomes the first stitch of the first ROW on one Side of the cosy. Slip the other half of the stitches onto a stitch holder (or another set of circular needles) while you work down one Side.

You could let the Zauberball do its own magic on the colouring with a simple stocking stitch. But I couldn't help myself. I balled the wool into two colours (MC and CC) and worked as follows:

Row 1: *P1 (MC), P1 (CC), repeat from * to end of row.
Row 2: *K1 (MC), K1 (CC), repeat from * to end of row.
Repeat the last 2 rows until the Side measures just below the spout and handle of your teapot.

Work the second Side the same. (I matched the colours closely to the first Side.) When you have the same number of rows on each Side of the tea cosy (COUNT the rows; don't rely on your 'Goodenuff'), proceed as follows.

Picot edge hem

With the right side facing, JOIN in the ROUND again, using Method 3 (see page 12).

Knit 9 rounds.

Rnd 10: *Yfwd, K2tog, repeat from * to end of round.
Rnd 11: Knit into every stitch to end of round.

𝒩ote. The yfwd becomes one large stitch and, as you knit into it, a lace hole forms.

Rnds 12–18: Knit.
Do NOT cast off.

Lining

Go to Basic Tea Cosy No 3 (see page 24), change to the sturdy 4-ply yarn, and work onwards from Continuing the Lining. This will give you a very neat Lining attached to the main cosy that will fold up beautifully inside the Outer Cosy.

Picot edge hem around spout and handle openings

This is a beautiful detail. Take the time. Push the Lining into the Outer Cosy. Sew the Lining to the Outer Cosy around the spout and handle openings.

With the right side facing – work in the ROUND. Using 3 mm (UK 11, USA 2/3) circular needles and Zauberball yarn, pick up stitches around the spout opening, about 1 stitch per row of knitting. Make sure that you have the same number of stitches (anything from 18 to 20 stitches) on either side of the opening.

Rnds 1 & 2: Knit.
Rnd 3: *Yfwd, K2tog, repeat from * to end of round.
Rnd 4: Knit into every stitch to end of round.
Rnds 5 & 6: Knit.
Cast off loosely.

Fold the hem back on itself to form the picot edge and sew into place.

Pillbox hat

With 3 mm (UK 11, USA 2/3) circular needles and Zauberball 100, knit as for the Upper Body (opposite), working the increasing pattern until there are 8 stitches fewer in total than you knitted in the Upper Body. For example, if the total number of stitches was 80 for the circumference of the Upper Body, the number of stitches for the circumference of the Pillbox Hat will be 72 in total. Proceed as follows:

Rnd 1: Knit.
Rnd 2: Purl.
Again, you could let the Zauberball do its own magic on the colouring with a simple stocking stitch. But I balled the wool into two colours (MC and CC) and did this:
Rnd 3: *K1 (MC), K1 (CC), repeat from * to end of round.
Rnd 4: *K1 (CC), K1 (MC), repeat from * to end of round.
Repeat the last 2 rounds 5 more times.
Rnd 15: Knit (MC). Stay with the main colour from now on.
Rnd 16: Purl.
Work the inside hem in stocking stitch, as follows:
Rnds 17–29: Knit.
Cast off loosely.

Frangipani flowers – make 6

Petal (make 5)

With 3 mm (UK 11, USA 2/3) circular needles and the apricot hues of Zauberball yarn, refer to Method 2, The Holy Cast-On (see page 10) to cast on 8 stitches.

Rnd 1: (K3, P1) twice.
Rnd 2: (K1, M1, <u>K1</u>, M1, K1, P1) twice (12 sts).
Rnd 3: (K5, P1) twice.
Rnd 4: (K2, M1, <u>K1</u>, M1, K2, P1) twice (16 sts).
Rnds 5 & 6: (K7, P1) twice.
Rnd 7: (K3, M1, <u>K1</u>, M1, K3, P1) twice (20 sts).
Rnds 8 & 9: (K9, P1) twice.
Rnd 10: (K2, ssk, <u>K1</u>, K2tog, K2, P1) twice (16 sts).
Rnds 11 & 12: (K7, P1) twice.
Rnd 13: (K1, ssk, <u>K1</u>, K2tog, K1, P1) twice (12 sts).
Rnds 14 & 15: (K5, P1) twice.
Rnd 16: (Ssk, <u>K1</u>, K2tog, P1) twice (8 sts).
Rnd 17: (K3, P1) twice.

Cut a long length of yarn and thread a darning needle. Thread the end yarn through the last 8 stitches.

The Holy Cast-On forms the outer tip of the Petal. The final drawing up of the stitches forms the point of contact with the other Petals in the centre of the flower.

The underlined <u>K1</u> forms the centre vein of the Petal. Line the veins up on either side of the Petal and, with your needle and thread, sew the back and front together down the vein.

Finishing the flowers

A light iron will make all the difference to the way the Petals and final flower sits. Do it. Sew all the Petals together with a small overlap at the centre point. Frangipanis always come in great bunches – so keep knitting.

Putting it all together

Cut the stiff interfacing to size to fit the Pillbox Hat. You need a circle crown and a straight rim interfacing. I used a plate of a similar size to mark out a circle and a ruler to measure the depth and length of the straight rim. Everyone's Pillbox Hat will be a little different, depending on the yarn you use and your tension.

Insert the circle interfacing into the crown of the Pillbox Hat and the straight interfacing into the rim. Turn the stocking stitch hem up inside the rim. Using a darning needle and the same coloured yarn as the Pillbox Hat crown edge, sew the hem into place taking care to hide the stitches in the knitting.

Put the cosy on the pot and, with the spout facing you, pin all the Frangipani Flowers off to one side and towards the front before you sew them into place. Très chic.

Hanging Pretty

Gorn. You have never seen a knitted coat hanger like this before, I bet.

FOR LINDA

MATERIALS

* 1 x 100 g (3½ oz) ball Schoppel Wolle Zauberball 100 yarn: Colour 1701 (Parrot) or Zauberball: Colour 2079 (Flower Garden) (see Note)
* 1 padded coat hanger

Note. Naturellement, there is a plethora of possibilities when choosing colours and accoutrements for your delectable coat hangers. You might have a matching coat hanger for every tea cosy in this little book. Ha. Now there's a challenge! For the red hanger, I used three different colours for knitting the garter stitch fabric: red, green and gold; and then five different colours (yes all from the same ball of Parrot yarn) for the weaving in.

EQUIPMENT

* Two sets 3 mm (UK 11, USA 2/3) circular needles, 80 cm (32 in) from tip to tip – Hanger Cover and Rolled Edge
* One set 2.75 mm (UK 12, USA 2) circular needles, 80 cm (32 in) from tip to tip – Hook Cover
* Darning needle

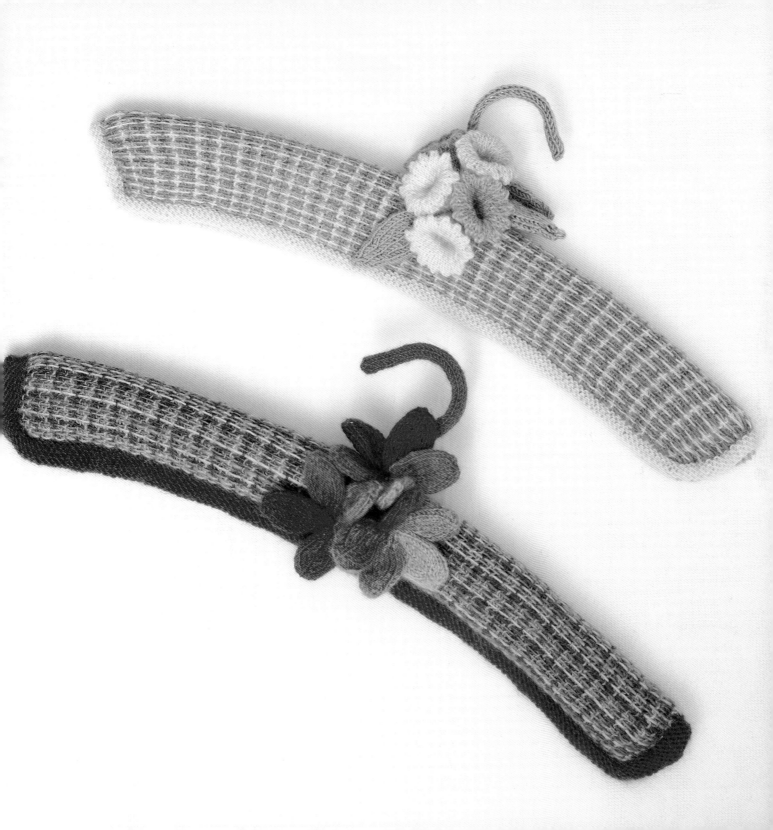

Hanger cover

Knitted in ROWS.

With 3 mm (UK 11, USA 2/3) circular needles and Red yarn, cast on 24 stitches. Knit one row. Join in the Green yarn and knit 2 rows. Join in the Gold yarn and knit 2 rows. Bring the Red yarn up and knit 2 rows. Bring the Green yarn up and knit 2 rows. Continue in this fashion until the cover measures the length of the hanger. Make sure it really does now. Stretching it to fit is not an option. Cast off.

Note. The edge with the yarns travelling up the side will be a little messy. Do your best to tighten the last stitch of each row as you begin the next – but don't fret too much – it will all be covered later on by the Rolled Edges.

Rolled edge

Start by picking up stitches on a long edge. The circular needles are very handy here. With the right side facing, using 3 mm (UK 11, USA 2/3) circular needles and Red yarn, pick up 1 stitch for each colour (1 stitch for every 2 rows) on a long edge. Pick up 1 stitch for each stitch on a short edge. Then, with the other set of circular needles, continue to pick up stitches for the second long and short edges.

You will be knitting in the ROUND with two SETS of circular needles. One SET of needles will hold half the stitches like a stitch holder. The other SET of needles will be working the other half of the stitches. Alternate between the two. There will always be a working set of needles and a sleeping set of needles. It is the yarn that goes round and round.

Purl every round for 5 rounds.

Cast off.

Preparing to weave

Lay the garter stitch fabric out lengthways in front of you, the way it will hang in the cupboard. Think of the fabric as having long HORIZONTAL rows and short (30 stitch) VERTICAL rows. You have already produced the vertical rows of Red, Green and Gold. Now, with a needle and yarn, you are going to weave in the horizontal rows of Red, Green and Gold and another two lighter shades of green and red.

Measure the first horizontal row of yarn out against the length of the hanger, adding a 5 cm (2 in) tail at both ends. Cut a bunch of threads to the same length in each of FIVE colours, ready to weave in.

Weaving

With a darning needle and Red wool, begin with a C row and weave OVER, under, over, under, and so on until the end of the row.

Note. Start every row drawing the yarn in from the back to the front of the work, before beginning the weaving process at the front of the work.

With the Green wool, begin the row immediately above the Red, which will be a ⊃ row, and weave UNDER, over, under, over and so on until the end of the row.

With the Gold wool, begin the row immediately above the Green, which will be a ⊂ row, and weave OVER, under, over, under and so on until the end of the row.

Cover the hanger

Measure the Cover against the hanger and find the point where the hook meets the hanger arc. Thread the hook through the knitted fabric and sew the front and back together just above the Rolled Edges.

Hem the Rolled Edges under.

Hook cover

With 2.75 mm (UK 12, USA 2) needles and Red yarn, refer to Method 2, The Holy Cast-On (see page 10) to cast on 8 stitches. Knit in the round until the length of the thin sock measures the same length as the hook. Cast off.

Frangipani flowers – make 3

With 3 mm (UK 11, USA 2/3) circular needles and Red yarn, make three Frangipani Flowers (see page 52).

Putting it all together

Thread the Hook cover over the hook and sew all the little bits and pieces to the hanger. Now isn't that just the prettiest thing?

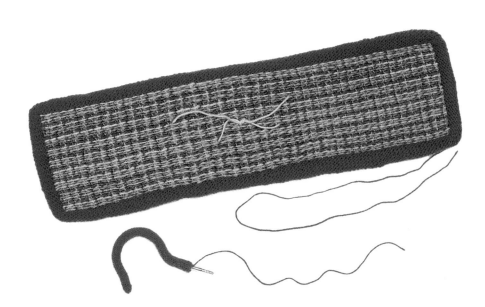

Happy Feet

What! You have never felt the sand between your toes wearing no-shoes?
You haven't LIVED girl, you haven't LIVED.

FOR THE GIRL WHO HAS EVERYTHING

MATERIALS
* 1 x 100 g (3½ oz) ball Schoppel Wolle Zauberball 100 yarn: Colour 1701 (Parrot)

EQUIPMENT
* One set 3 mm (UK 11, USA 2/3) circular needles, 80 cm (32 in) from tip to tip – Flowers
* One pair 4 mm (UK 8, USA 6) double-pointed needles – I-cord
* Darning needle
* Scissors

I-cord — make 2

Use the greens and blues for the i-cord straps.

With 4 mm (UK 8, USA 6) double-pointed needles and two strands of Zauberball 100, cast on 3 stitches. Work i-cord (see page 15) for 60 cm (23½ in) or until long enough to fit around the toe and tie in a bow at the back of the heel.

Frangipani flowers — make 4

Use the oranges and yellows for the frangipanis.

With 3 mm (UK 11, USA 2/3) circular needles and Zauberball 100, make four frangipanis (see page 52), two for each No-Shoe.

Putting it all together

Fold the i-cords in half and, with darning needle and yarn, stitch the i-cords together for a distance up the arch of the foot, leaving room at the loop end for the toe to pop through. Secure the Frangipanis with a few firm stitches to the joined section of i-cord.

Fruitopia

My big sister, Rhonda, knitted all this fruit. And the base. And lining. Oh yeah, and the three basic tea cosies at the front of the book there (each one importantly, subtly different from the others). That's right, and heaps of those little bell flowers and leaves for Just an Old-Fashioned Girl. Well, she did ask if she could help. And what are big sisters for if they aren't for helping?

Fruitopia, for my big sister, Rhonda. No, you can't have her after she's been photographed. She has work to do, showing off her lusciousness to thousands of adoring tea cosy fans around the country. Hey Wowa, can you knit me up a couple more Fruitopias, please? Pweeeese. For your Onnie. Gorn.

SIZE

To fit a six-cup teapot that stands 13 cm (5 in) tall (not including the knob) and 15 cm (6 in) in diameter (not including the spout and handle). Choose a large round teapot with a flattish curved top. The Flight Cap needs to sit down over the bowl of the teapot.

MATERIALS

* 6 x 50 g (1¾ oz) balls Noro Silk Garden Lite yarn – Cosy Base, Flight Cap and Fruit (choose your colours carefully, remembering you need green, orange, pink, red, purple and yellow/brown)
* 1 x 50 g (1¾ oz) ball of any sturdy 8-ply yarn – Lining
* 30 cm (12 in) square very stiff interfacing – Flight Cap
* Drawing paper to make the Flight Cap interfacing template
* Polyester fibrefill

EQUIPMENT

* One set 4 mm (UK 8, USA 6) circular needles, 100 cm (40 in) from tip to tip

METHOD

Cosy Base and Lining are knitted in the round from the top down. Chequered Band is knitted in the round. Leaf-shaped Tray is knitted in rows.

Cosy base

With 4 mm (UK 8, USA 6) circular needles and Noro Silk Garden Lite yarn, make the Basic Tea Cosy No 1 (see page 20).

Lining

YES. Absolutely you need a lining. Again, use the Basic Tea Cosy No 1, with 4 mm (UK 8, USA 6) circular needles and any sturdy 8-ply yarn of similar hue to the yarn you used for the Cosy Base.

Flight cap

The Flight Cap is knitted in two parts, the Chequered Band with the inside hem, and the Leaf-shaped Tray, to carry the fruit.

Chequered band

Ball the Noro into its obvious colours. Choose six colours (C1, C2, C3, C4, C5, C6), two for each block of colour work.

With 4 mm (UK 8, USA 6) circular needles and C1, cast on 112 (+ 1) stitches, join in the round with Method 1 (see page 9). Work from the Graph (below), or knit as follows:

Rnd 1: *K4 (C1), K4 (C2), repeat from * to end of round. Repeat Rnd 1 four more times (5 rounds in total).
Rnd 6: *K4 (C3), K4 (C4), repeat from * to end of round. Repeat Rnd 6 four more times (5 rounds in total).
Rnd 11: *K4 (C5), K4 (C6), repeat from * to end of round. Repeat Rnd 11 four more times (5 rounds in total).
Rnd 16: (Drop the darker colour of the two you have just used and continue with the lighter colour.) Knit.
Rnd 17: Purl.
Rnds 18–35: Knit.
Cast off.

Chequered Band Graph

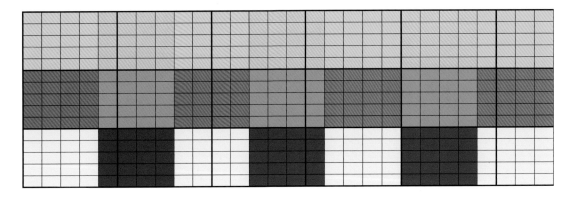

Leaf-shaped tray

Use your least favourite colour to knit this last bit. It will be hidden by all the delicious fare on top.

With 4 mm (UK 8, USA 6) circular needles and Noro Silk Garden Lite, cast on 5 stitches. Do not join in the round – you are knitting in ROWS. The underlined <u>K1</u> marks the middle point of the work.

Row 1 (and each alternate row): Purl.
Row 2: K2, M1, <u>K1</u>, M1, K2 (7 sts).
Row 4: K3, M1, <u>K1</u>, M1, K3 (9 sts).
Row 6: K4, M1, <u>K1</u>, M1, K4 (11 sts).
Row 8: K5, M1, <u>K1</u>, M1, K5 (13 sts).
Row 10: K6, M1, <u>K1</u>, M1, K6 (15 sts).
Row 12: K4, M1, knit to last 4 stitches, M1, K4 (17 sts).
Row 13: Purl.
Repeat last 2 rows 8 more times (33 sts).
Row 30: Knit.
Row 31: Purl.
Repeat last 2 rows 9 more times.
Row 50: K4, ssk, knit to the last 6 stitches, K2tog, K4 (31 sts).
Row 51: Purl.
Repeat last 2 rows 7 more times (17 sts).
Row 66: K6, ssk, <u>K1</u>, K2tog, K6 (15 sts).
Row 67 (and each alternate row): Purl.
Row 68: K5, ssk, <u>K1</u>, K2tog, K5.
Row 70: K4, ssk, <u>K1</u>, K2tog, K4.
Row 72: K3, ssk, <u>K1</u>, K2tog, K3.
Row 74: K2, ssk, <u>K1</u>, K2tog, K2.
Row 76: K1, ssk, <u>K1</u>, K2tog, K1 (5 sts).
Row 77: Purl.
Cast off.

Fruit

Make 1 Pear, 1 green Apple, 2 Mandarins, lots of Strawberries and lots of Grapes (see pages 67–73). But if this isn't enough to burst out the top of the Flight Cap, MAKE MORE.

Putting it all together

Colour work always sits better after blocking. Take the time to wet the knitted fabric of the Chequered Band through, squeeze out all the excess water and lay flat to dry. Noro yarn SMELLS like sheep, so wet it for a whiff of the country.

When the Chequered Band is dry, use the purl row as your folding edge. Fold the plain band down inside the Chequered Band. Lay it flat on the drawing paper. Curve the band slightly, drawing the bottom stitches in closer to each other and stretching the top stitches out a little. Pencil an outline around the band. Set the band aside and cut out the template. From the template cut two very stiff interfacing inserts. Carefully round off all the corners of the inserts so they don't poke through the knitted fabric. Pin and sew the band around the bottom to keep the inserts in place.

To complete the Flight Cap, pin and sew the Leaf-shaped Tray to the inside of the Chequered Band, about 1 cm (3/8 in) from the top all the way round.

Place the Lining inside the Cosy Base and sew together around the spout and handle openings. Dress the teapot with the Lining and Cosy. Place the Flight Cap on top of the pot but do not secure it to the Cosy Base just yet. Place all the fruit in the Flight Cap the way you'd like to see it. Remove all the fruit, bar the back piece, the Pear (opposite). With needle and yarn, sew the Pear into place with only a couple of stitches. Place all the fruit in the Flight Cap again. Then remove all, bar the Pear and one more piece, the Apple. Sew the Apple into place. Continue to dress the entire thing before removing and sewing on one more piece of fruit. That way, you will achieve the most beautifully arranged fruit hat in the Southern Hemisphere, or the Northern Hemisphere, or wherever you are.

Once all the fruit is in place, you can secure the fruity Flight Cap to the Cosy Base with a couple of stitches at the front and a couple more at the back of the cap.

Tutti Frutti Ears

Please do wear any of the fruit dangling from your ears but only if you are old and eccentric and used to being seen out and about in unusual attire. Otherwise, stick to the strawberry danglers please. And be sure to wear these with great aplomb.

MATERIALS

* Noro Silk Garden Lite yarn (balled into Red and Green hues)
* Polyester fibrefill
* Earring findings or head pins

EQUIPMENT

* One set 4 mm (UK 8, USA 6) (or 3.5 mm, UK 9/10, USA 4, if you are a loose knitter) circular needles, 80 cm (32 in) from tip to tip
* Darning needle
* One pair 4 mm (UK 8, USA 6) double-pointed needles (for i-cord)
* Pointy-nosed jewellery pliers

Strawberry — make 2

With 4 mm (UK 8, USA 6) circular needles and Noro Silk Garden Lite (red hues), refer to Method 2, The Holy Cast-On (see page 10) to cast on 6 stitches.

Rnd 1: Knit.
Rnd 2: *K1, increase once in the next stitch (by knitting into the front and back of it), repeat from * to end of round (9 sts).
Rnd 3: Knit.
Rnd 4: *K3, M1, repeat from * to end of round (12 sts).
Rnd 5: Knit.
Rnd 6: *K4, M1, repeat from * to end of round (15 sts).
Rnd 7: Knit.
The stitches will be unevenly distributed across the needles at this point. Redistribute them evenly if you feel the need.
Rnd 8: *K5, M1, repeat from * to end of round (18 sts).
Rnd 9: Knit.
Rnd 10: *K3, M1, repeat from * to end of round (24 sts).
Rnd 11: Knit.
Rnd 12: *K4, M1, repeat from * to end of round (30 sts).
Rnd 13: Knit.
Time to add in the leafy green.

Rnd 14: K2 (Red), K1 (Green), *K4 (Red), K1 (Green), repeat from * to last 2 sts, K2 (Red).
Rnd 15: K1 (Red), *K3 (Green), K2 (Red), repeat from * to last 4 sts, K3 (Green), K1 (Red).
Break off Red and continue in Green only:
Rnd 16: Knit.
Rnd 17: *K3, K2tog, repeat from * to end of round (24 sts).
Rnd 18: Knit.
Rnd 19: *K2tog, repeat from * to end of round (12 sts).
Fill and shape with fibrefill but not to the brim.
Rnd 20: *K2tog, repeat from * to end of round (6 sts).
Rnd 21: *K1, K2tog, repeat from * to end of round (4 sts).

Place the 4 remaining stitches onto a 4 mm (UK 8, USA 6) double-pointed needle and continue in i-cord (see page 15) for 1.5 cm (5/8 in), to create a stalk. Thread yarn through last 4 stitches and draw up tight.

Putting it all together

Attach your Strawberries to your earring findings, or bend the head pins into hook shapes, thread on the fruit, pop them in your ears, shake your head in a carefree manner and off you go!

More fruit

All the fruit is made with the delicious, the delectable, Noro Silk Garden Lite. You could use any 8-ply (DK) yarn but if you'd like your fruit to look like the fruit in the picture, this is not the moment to be frugal. You'll buy more yardage of yarn than you need to get the colours you want. Noro changes its colour charts constantly. Look at the current palette and choose well.

MATERIALS

✽ Noro Silk Garden Lite yarn
✽ Polyester fibrefill

EQUIPMENT

✽ One set 4 mm (UK 8, USA 6) (or 3.5 mm, UK 9/10, USA 4, if you are a loose knitter) circular needles, 80 cm (32 in) from tip to tip
✽ Darning needle
✽ One pair 4 mm (UK 8, USA 6) double-pointed needles (for i-cord)

Grape

With 4 mm (UK 8, USA 6) circular needles and Noro Silk Garden Lite, refer to Method 2, The Holy Cast-On (see page 10) to cast on 8 stitches.

Rnd 1: Knit.
Rnd 2: Increase once in every stitch (by knitting into the front and back of it) to end of round (16 sts).
Rnds 3 & 4: Knit.
Rnd 5: *K1, increase once in next stitch, repeat from * to end of round (24 sts).
Rnds 6 & 7: Knit.
Rnd 8: *K1, K2tog, repeat from * to end of round (16 sts).
Rnds 9 & 10: Knit.
Rnd 11: *K2tog, repeat from * to end of round (8 sts).
Rnd 12: Knit.
Fill with fibrefill, not too much and not too little, just right.

Cut off a long thread and, with a darning needle, draw closed the remaining 8 stitches. Sew a couple of stitches to hold in place.

Apple / Mandarin

With 4 mm (UK 8, USA 6) circular needles and Noro Silk Garden Lite, refer to Method 2, The Holy Cast-On (see page 10) to cast on 8 stitches.

Rnd 1: Knit.
Rnd 2: Increase once in every stitch (by knitting into the front and back of it) to end of round (16 sts).
Rnd 3: Knit.
Rnd 4: *K1, increase once in next stitch, repeat from * to end of round (24 sts).
Rnd 5: Knit.
Rnd 6: *K2, increase once in next stitch, repeat from * to end of round (32 sts).
Rnds 7 & 8: Knit.
Rnd 9: *K4, M1, repeat from * to end of round (40 sts).
Rnds 10 & 11: Knit.
Rnd 12: *K5, M1, repeat from * to end of round (48 sts).
Mandarin only: Knit 6 rounds without shaping.

Apple only: Knit 8 rounds without shaping.
Both fruits: Start the round count again at number 1, as follows:
Rnd 1: *K4, K2tog, repeat from * to end of round (40 sts).
Rnds 2 & 3: Knit.
Rnd 4: *K3, K2tog, repeat from * to end of round (32 sts).
Rnds 5 & 6: Knit.
Rnd 7: *K2, K2tog, repeat from * to end of round (24 sts).
Rnd 8: Knit.
Rnd 9: *K1, K2tog, repeat from * to end of round (16 sts).
Rnd 10: Knit.
Fill and shape with fibrefill but not to the brim.
Rnd 11: *K2tog, repeat from * to end of round (8 sts).
Rnd 12: Knit.
Fill the remaining space with fibrefill, not too much, not too little, just right.

Cut off a long thread and, with a darning needle, draw closed the remaining 8 stitches. Poke the needle all the way through from cast-off to cast-on point, draw up the thread a little to make the shape of an apple or mandarin. Make a couple of holding stitches there and poke the needle back up through the middle of the fruit to the top and make a couple of holding stitches there too.

Apple stem

With 4 mm (UK 8, USA 6) double-pointed needles and Noro Silk Garden Lite, make a 2 cm (¾ in) long i-cord (see page 15) for the Apple Stem.

Apple leaf

With 4 mm (UK 8, USA 6) circular needles and Noro Silk Garden Lite, refer to Method 2, The Holy Cast-On (see page 10) to cast on 8 stitches. Don't pull up as tightly as you might for the fruit. You are making a flat leaf, not a peachy apple.

Rnd 1: (K3, P1) twice.
Rnd 2: (K1, M1, <u>K1</u>, M1, K1, P1) twice (12 sts).
Rnd 3: (K5, P1) twice.
Rnd 4: (K2, M1, <u>K1</u>, M1, K2, P1) twice (16 sts).
Rnds 5 & 6: Knit.
Rnd 7: (K1, ssk, <u>K1</u>, K2tog, K1, P1) twice (12 sts).
Rnds 8 & 9: Knit.
Rnd 10: (Ssk, <u>K1</u>, K2tog, P1) twice (8 sts).
Rnd 11: (K3, P1) twice.
Rnd 12: (Ssk, ssk) twice (4 sts).

Cut off a long thread and, with a darning needle, draw closed the remaining 4 stitches. The underlined K1 forms the centre vein of the Leaf. Line the veins up on either side of the Leaf and, with your needle and thread, sew the back and front together down the vein.

Putting it all together

Catch the Stem and Leaf to the top of the Apple with a couple of stitches in matching thread.

Pear

With 4 mm (UK 8, USA 6) circular needles and Noro Silk Garden Lite, refer to Method 2, The Holy Cast-On (see page 10) to cast on 8 stitches.

Rnd 1: Knit.
Rnd 2: Increase once in every stitch (by knitting into the front and back of it) to end of round (16 sts).
Rnd 3: Knit.
Rnd 4: *K1, increase once in next stitch, repeat from * to end of round (24 sts).
Rnd 5: Knit.
Rnd 6: *K2, increase once in next stitch, repeat from * to end of round (32 sts).
Rnd 7: Knit.
Rnd 8: *K3, increase once in next stitch, repeat from * to end of round (40 sts).
Rnds 9–11: Knit.
Rnd 12: *K5, M1, repeat from * to end of round (48 sts).
Rnds 13–18: Knit.
Rnd 19: *K4, K2tog, repeat from * to end of round (40 sts).
Rnds 20–22: Knit.
Rnd 23: *K3, K2tog, repeat from * to end of round (32 sts).
Rnds 24 & 25: Knit.
Rnd 26: *K2, K2tog, repeat from * to end of round (24 sts).
Rnd 27: Knit.
Rnd 28: *K1, K2tog, repeat from * to end of round (16 sts).

Fill and shape with fibrefill but not to the brim.
Rnds 29–33: Knit.
Rnd 34: *K4, M1, repeat from * to end of round (20 sts).
Rnd 35: Knit.
Rnd 36: *K2, K2tog, repeat from * to end of round (15 sts).
Rnd 37: *K1, K2tog, repeat from * to end of round (10 sts).
Fill and shape with fibrefill to the brim.
Rnd 38: *K2tog, repeat from * to end of round (5 sts).

Cut off a long thread and, with a darning needle, draw closed the remaining 5 stitches. Poke the needle all the way through from cast-off to cast-on point, draw up a little to make the shape of a pear. Make a couple of holding stitches there and poke the needle back up through the middle of the fruit to the top and make a couple of holding stitches there too.

Pear stem

Make as for Apple Stem (see page 71).

Putting it all together

Catch Stem to top of Pear with a couple of stitches.

She's Apples

A variation on the theme of Fruitopia (see page 60). One discovered the Rustic Basket Stitch pattern, which wasn't called the Rustic Basket Stitch pattern in the place that One discovered it. One discovered it just days before One was to hand in the final patterns for edit. One HAD to use it, so One whipped up She's Apples. One hopes you are as pleased with it as One is.

SIZE

To fit a four-cup teapot that stands 11 cm (4¼ in) tall (not including the knob) and 14 cm (5½ in) in diameter (not including the spout and handle).

MATERIALS

* 2 x 50 g (1¾ oz) balls any Aran tweed or Aran DK yarn – Rustic Basket and Lining (see Note)
* 1 x 50 g (1¾ oz) ball Noro Silk Garden Lite yarn (choose your colours well now – I made green apples and red strawberries, but of course apples come in a number of apple colours)
* Enough polyester fibrefill to stuff fruit

Note. I used one each of Debbie Bliss Donegal Luxury Tweed Aran yarn, Main Colour (MC): 36 (Gold), which is more a Mustard colour really, and Brooklyn Tweed Shelter yarn, Contrast Colour (CC): 17 (Embers), which is a Rusty Brown.

EQUIPMENT

* Two sets 4 mm (UK 8, USA 6) circular needles, 80 cm (32 in) from tip to tip (see Another note)
* Darning needle
* Scissors
* Small to medium crochet hook

Another note. The second set is used to help rearrange stitches when moving from double knitting to knitting in the round with the Magic Loop and back again.

METHOD

A little bit of very easy double knitting: don't fret.

Knitting in the round with the Magic Loop.

Rustic basket cosy/lining
Basket sides (make 2)

Note. The pattern starts at the bottom of the Basket and uses the double knitting method to knit the front and back of the Basket Sides at the same time – backwards and forwards in rows. This method gives a nice stretchy seam along the bottom. It also provides an opportunity to understand what double knitting is and how it works.

Bottom band
Begun with double knitting.

With 4 mm (UK 8, USA 6) circular needles and Debbie Bliss Tweed Aran (MC), cast on 70 stitches. (Yes, you are working in ROWS but use the circular needles. You need them to work in ROUNDS later on.)

Another note. It is essential that you pay attention to the placement of your yarn while double knitting. All will become clear.

Row 1 (front): *Yarn back, K1, yfwd, slip 1 purlwise, repeat from * to end of row.
Row 2 (back): *Yarn back, K1, yfwd, slip 1 purlwise, repeat from * to end of row.
Repeat Rows 1 and 2 three more times (8 rows in all).

Final note. If you accidentally purl the stitch instead of only SLIPPING it purlwise, you will join the front and back fabrics together. Usually a big no no, but in this case, not such a sin, as the two fabrics don't need to open up, as they do in Un Joli Petit Cadeau (see page 42).

Setting up to knit in the round with the Magic Loop

To separate the front and back fabrics of the double knitting, hold the second set of circular needles in one hand as a pair and slip the stitches from the working needle onto the extra set, a stitch from the front onto the front needle, a stitch from the back onto the back needle, back and forth to the end of the row. You should now have all the stitches from the back fabric on one half of the extra circular needles and all the stitches from the front fabric on the other half.

Now the front and back fabrics are separated. But! The working thread is sitting in the middle of the extra set of circular needles. Slip the stitches back onto the original set of circular needles leaving a loop in the cable, with 35 stitches on each half.

Now, off you go with the Rustic Basket Stitch pattern.

Rustic basket stitch pattern

The Rustic Basket Stitch pattern is worked over 12 rounds and is made up of knit stitches and Drop Stitches and two different coloured yarns.

Drop Stitch (Drop1)

Drop the next stitch off the needle and unravel 4 rows down. Insert the working needle into the MC (Mustard) stitch in the round below, front to back, and knit, catching the 4 loose strands of CC (Rusty Brown) at the back.

𝓝ote. In this pattern, the Rustic Basket Stitch is only worked on half the stitches of the round, forming the Outer Cosy. The second half of the stitches are simply knitted, forming the cosy Lining.

Rnds 1–4: Using CC (Rusty Brown), knit.
Rnd 5: Using MC (Mustard), K1, *Drop1, K3, repeat from * to last 2 stitches of Outer Cosy (that is, half the round, 35 sts), Drop1, K1; knit to end of round.
Rnd 6: Using MC, knit to end of round.
Rnds 7–10: Using CC, knit.
Rnd 11: Using MC, K3, *Drop1, K3, repeat from * to end of Outer Cosy; knit to end of round.
Rnd 12: Using MC, knit to end of round.
Repeat these 12 rounds two more times.

And then repeat Rounds 1–6.

There should be 7 rows of rustic basket 'bumps'.

Setting up to double knit the top band

This really is worth the effort so that the Top Band sits the same way as the Bottom Band. You'll need that extra set of circular needles again.

Move all the stitches up onto the needles, the front stitches on the front needle and the back stitches on the back needle. With one needle tip of the extra set of 4 mm (UK 8, USA 6) circular needles, slip one stitch from the front 'holding' needle and one stitch from the back 'holding' needle. Continue to slip, front stitch and then back stitch alternately until all 70 stitches are set up in a ROW on the extra set of needles, front back, front back.

We are ready to return to double knitting:

Row 1 (front): *Yarn back, K1, yfwd, slip 1 purlwise, repeat from * to end of row.
Row 2 (back): *Yarn back, K1, yfwd, slip 1 purlwise, repeat from * to end of row.
Repeat Rows 1 and 2 once more (4 rows in all).

Casting off

Knit 1, bring the yarn forward and slip 1 purlwise, take the yarn back and knit 1. Pick up the back two stitches on the working needle and bring up and over the third stitch to cast off.

With the yarn forward, slip 1 purlwise, with the yarn back, knit 1. Pick up the back two stitches on the working needle over the front one to cast off.

Continue the last instruction to the last stitch. Purl. Cast off the last two stitches.

Tighten any loose threads and, with a crochet hook, hide them inside the double fabric.

Sew the Basket Sides together below and above the spout and handle. Plonk it on the teapot. Now you can measure the diameter for the Apple Holding Tray. The Apple Holding Tray sits at the top of the Rusty Brown bumps (on the inside naturally) and below the Mustard double knit Top Band.

Apple holding tray

Go to the Basic Tea Cosy No 1 (see page 20). Work the pattern to the end of the Upper Body. MEASURE it against the Rustic Basket Cosy on the teapot and continue increasing until you think it fits. Cast off.

Apple – make 3

See pages 70–1.

Strawberry – make 2

See page 68.

Putting it all together

Sew the Apple Holding Tray in position. Place the fruit just so and stitch to the bottom of the Apple Holding Tray. Funny that.

She's Apples!

Heart Throb

My heart throbs with the love of double knitting. Its practice is sooo ... therapeutic ... in the way it focuses the mind and is so satisfying in its execution. I feel particularly accomplished when I double knit.

DOUBLE KNITTING

Double knitting is a clever technique where back-to-back fabrics are knitted simultaneously, using two threads working in ROWS on ONE pair of needles. You get reversible knitting, double thickness, with stocking stitch on both sides.

If you have never done double knitting before, begin with the EASY square, the Square of Squares. Trust me. This is very valuable advice.

If you are a watcher rather than a reader, then Google YouTube, Double Knitting, and take a tutorial – there are lots.

SIZE

To fit a six-cup teapot that stands 13 cm (5 in) tall (not including the knob) and 15 cm (6 in) in diameter (not including the spout and handle).

MATERIALS

Any two colours of 8-ply (DK) yarn will do beautifully for this project (see Note)

Note. I used a Cascade 220 yarn, Main Colour (MC): (Pink) and a Brooklyn Tweed Shelter yarn, Contrast Colour (CC): 28 (Sweatshirt), which is Grey. There are exactly 100 g (3½ oz) of yarn in my cosy. If it were me, I'd be buying more than 50 g (1¾ oz) of each colour to be sure of making it to the end. You can never have too much yarn.

EQUIPMENT

* One set 6 mm (UK 3, USA 10½) (or 5.5 mm (UK 5, USA 9) if you are a loose knitter) circular needles, 80 cm (32 in) from tip to tip – the squares are knitted on the straight in ROWS
* One set 4 mm (UK 8, USA 6) circular needles, 80 cm (32 in) from tip to tip (used for the cast-on only)
* Darning needle
* Scissors
* Pompom maker

Square of squares

You need to make two Squares, one each for the Front and Back of your cosy, one with a Heart and one with Little Squares. One side of the double-knitted square will be edged in the main colour (see the Graphs on pages 148–151) – Pink heart, Pink edging, Pink mini squares, Pink edging.

With 4 mm (UK 8, USA 6) circular needles and MC (Pink) yarn, cast on 71 stitches.

Change to the 6 mm (UK 3, USA 10½) circular needles. Remember, you are knitting in ROWS.

Row 1: Purl the first stitch with MC (Pink). This is the Pink side edging.

Useful tip. Pull the working yarn downwards after making the first stitch of the row to tighten the stitch on the row below. Do this after making the first stitch of every row.

Take MC to the back. Knit the next stitch with CC (Grey). Don't tie the Grey in. Just pick it up and start. You can hide the end bit through the middle of the front and back fabrics later on.

And off we go – bring both yarns forward, purl with MC only, both yarns back, knit with CC only, both yarns forward, purl with MC only, both yarns back, knit with CC only. All the way to the last stitch. Both yarns forward, purl with MC only.

Row 2: Both yarns back, knit with MC only …

Very important note. After making the first stitch, twist the Pink and Grey yarns around each other so that they catch before making the second stitch. This will ensure that the front and back fabrics are joined at the edges. Do this after making the first stitch at the beginning of every row.

… both yarns forward, purl with CC only, pull the yarn downwards to tighten the first of the CC (Grey) stitches on the row below, take both yarns back, knit with MC only, bring both yarns forward, purl with CC only. Take both yarns back, knit with MC only. Bring both yarns forward, purl with CC only. All the way to the last stitch. Take both yarns back, knit with MC only.

You are on your way! All you have to do now is follow the pattern Graphs (one Graph for each Side of the cosy, see pages 148–151).

Three very helpful tips ...

1. When counting rows in a Graph pattern, always count the row on the needles.

2. Always start the picture pattern (the Squares or the Heart), with the Grey surrounded by the Pink edging facing you.

3. COUNT the stitches on the needle in pairs, like this: One AND, two AND, three AND – 'one' being the knit stitch of the front fabric, 'AND' being the purl stitch of the back fabric. Etc. Then, when you come to change colours from front to back, there will be less confusion.

Preparing for blast-off – sorry, CAST-off

There is a Preparation Row before casting off, as follows:

With the Pink squares and the Pink edging facing and both yarns forward, purl the Pink only. Take both yarns back and knit with the PINK only. Yes, Pink. Bring both yarns forward and SLIP the next stitch purlwise, take both yarns back and knit with the PINK only, bring both yarns forward and SLIP the next stitch purlwise. After working 8 pairs of stitches, cut the Grey yarn, but leave it out the back to pull tight later.

There should only be PINK stitches on the working needles. By SLIPPING the stitches of the back fabric (not purling them) you maintain the double fabric separation. Continue until the last stitch. Purl.

Casting off

Knit, bring the yarn forward and slip purlwise, take the yarn back and knit. Pick up the back two stitches on the working needle and bring up and over the third stitch to cast off.

With the yarn forward, slip purlwise, with the yarn back, knit. Pick up the back two stitches on the working needle over the front one to cast off.

Continue the last instruction to the last stitch. Purl. Cast off the last two stitches.

Tighten any loose threads and, with a crochet hook, hide them inside the double fabric.

Pompoms

Make four little pink pompoms to sit two atop each of the squares.

Putting it all together

Sew the pompoms to the upper corners of the squares. I have pinched the two squares together with a (hidden) stitch about 5 cm (2 in) diagonally in from the corners. Pin it together first and try it on the pot. See how the bottom splays out from the teapot and the top corners fall open showing off your double-sided knitting. Gorgeous Porgeous.

Hot Potatoes

Gorn. You have to admit. Those double knit squares make great pot holders. Choose your preferred pattern from the graphs and double knit into the night. Add a length of i-cord and Bob's your uncle. He really IS your uncle? There you go then.

Check out the rest of the information from Heart Throb (see page 80) and see the Graphs on pages 152–153.

OK, so you want to know what I did. I used a Brooklyn Tweed Shelter yarn, Main Colour (MC): 07 (Thistle), which is a plum-coloured Purple, and Jo Sharp Silkroad DK Tweed, Contrast Colour 1 (CC1): 426 (Asparagus), which is the darker Green, and Jo Sharp Silkroad DK Tweed, Contrast Colour 2 (CC2): 427 (Lime), which is the lighter Green.

Of course, you could make matching tea cosy and pot holders …

Double Knit Neck Warmer
with Woven Windows

I first saw double knitting worn around someone's gorgeous neck at a Textile Forum in Geelong. Boy, was I impressed. With the scarf. And clearly the neck too. I'd never seen anything like it anywhere, the scarf that is, the double knitted scarf.

It IS possible to have One's head in the sand, even though One considers Oneself to be reasonably social media savvy. Since seeing what One saw in real life that day and adding One's own rich sauce to the pasta, and sticking it up as a freebie on the blog, One has seen similar things on Ravelry, but never with the Woven Window. So One is claiming that as One's own, and the choice of yarn, and the crocheted edging and the love, definitely the love.

DOUBLE KNITTING

Before you tackle this, read the other little bit under the Double Knitting in the Heart Throb tea cosy pattern on page 80, but I'm going to put the three very helpful hints (page 83) here again, plus another one.

Four very helpful tips ...

1. When counting rows in a Graph pattern, always count the row on the needles.

2. Always start the picture pattern (the Windows to Weave), with the Pink surrounded by the Green edging facing you.

3. COUNT the stitches on the needle in pairs, like this: One AND, two AND, three AND – 'one' being the knit stitch of the front fabric, 'AND' being the purl stitch of the back fabric. Etc. Then, when you come to change colours from front to back, there will be less confusion.

4. I have used the terms 'Green' and 'Pink' for reference to the graph only. You will need to keep a firm grasp on the varied colours of the Noro wool appearing in front of you as you knit.

SIZE

Length: 1.5 m (5 ft)
Width: 23 cm (9 in)

MATERIALS

* 3 x 50 g (1¾ oz) balls Noro Silk Garden Lite yarn (of the one hue, say Green): MC
* 3 x 50 g (1¾ oz) balls Noro Silk Garden Lite yarn (of a contrasting hue, say Pink): CC

EQUIPMENT

* One set 6 mm (UK 3, USA 10½) (or 5.5 mm (UK 5, USA 9) if you are a loose knitter) circular needles, 80 cm (32 in) from tip to tip – the scarf is knitted on the straight in ROWS
* One set 4 mm (UK 8, USA 6) circular needles, 80 cm (32 in) from tip to tip (used for the cast-on only)
* One 4 mm (UK 8, USA G/6) crochet hook (used for the chain stitch edging)
* Darning needle
* Scissors

Neck warmer

Setting up the pattern

With 4 mm (UK 8, USA 6) circular needles and MC (Green) yarn, cast on 68 stitches (35 for the back and 33 for the front).

Change to the 6 mm (UK 3, USA 10½) circular needles. Remember, you are knitting in ROWS.

Row 1: Purl the first stitch with MC (Green). This is the Green side edging.

Useful tip. Pull the working yarn downwards after making the first stitch of the row to tighten the stitch on the row below. Do this after making the first stitch of every row.

Take MC to the back. Knit the next stitch with CC (Pink). Don't tie the Pink in. Just pick it up and start. You can hide the end bit through the middle of the front and back fabrics later on.

And off we go – bring both yarns forward, purl with MC only, both yarns back, knit with CC only, both yarns forward, purl with MC only, both yarns back, knit with CC only. All the way to the last stitch. Both yarns forward, purl with MC only.

Row 2: Both yarns back, knit with MC only ...

Very important note. After making the first stitch, twist the Green and Pink yarns around each other so that they catch before making the second stitch. This will ensure that the front and back fabrics are joined at the edges. Do this after making the first stitch at the beginning of every row.

... both yarns forward, purl with CC only, pull the yarn downwards to tighten the first of the CC (Pink) stitches on the row below, take both yarns back, knit with MC (Green) only, bring both yarns forward, purl with CC only. Take both yarns back, knit with MC only. Bring both yarns forward, purl with CC only. All the way to the last stitch. Take both yarns back, knit with MC only.

You are on your way! All you have to do now is follow the pattern Graphs (one Graph for each Side of the Neck Warmer – on pages 154–155) until you reach the desired length.

Preparing for cast-off

There is a Preparation Row before casting off, as follows:

With the Green squares and the Green edging facing and both yarns forward, purl the Green only. Take both yarns back and knit with the GREEN only. Yes, Green. Bring both yarns forward and SLIP the next stitch purlwise, take both yarns back and knit with the GREEN only, bring both yarns forward and SLIP the next stitch purlwise. After working 8 pairs of stitches, cut the Pink yarn, but leave it out the back to pull tight later.

There should only be GREEN stitches on the working needles. By SLIPPING the stitches of the back fabric (not purling them) you maintain the double fabric separation. Continue until the last stitch. Purl.

Casting off

Knit, bring the yarn forward and slip purlwise, take the yarn back and knit. Pick up the back two stitches on the working needle and bring up and over the third stitch to cast off.

With the yarn forward, slip purlwise, with the yarn back, knit. Pick up the back two stitches on the working needle over the front one to cast off.

Continue the last instruction to the last stitch. Purl. Cast off the last two stitches.

Tighten any loose threads and, with a crochet hook, hide them inside the double fabric.

Edging

The crochet edge is a nice way to tidy up the double knit edge. Using the 4 mm (UK 8, USA G/6) crochet hook and the colour of your choice, slipstitch into the edge of the neck warmer. Chain for 5, miss a row or two of knitting and slipstitch again. Make it up as you go along. Keep it simple.

Weaving

You have created the wrong side of stocking stitch in the little windows. This is different from the garter stitch set up for the weaving described on page 16 but the principle is exactly the same. Over, under, over, under each bump of the purl stitches in each column.

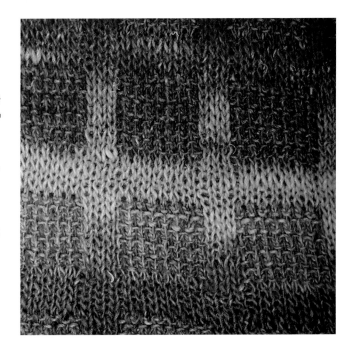

Cheroot and Chai

You might recognise the fez, previously incarnated as a Pillbox Hat in Hawaiian Beauty (see page 48) and, yes, very clever of you, as Beatrice and Eugenie in How Tea Cosies Changed the World. Now see how a new yarn and a fancy embellishment can make the same thing so completely different.

FOR ANNE OF MELBOURNE

SIZE

To fit a four-cup teapot that stands 11 cm (4¼ in) tall (not including the knob) and 14 cm (5½ in) in diameter (not including the spout and handle).

MATERIALS

* 2 x 50 g (1¾ oz) balls Noro Silk Garden Lite yarn
* 30 cm (12 in) square stiff interfacing

EQUIPMENT

* One set 4 mm (UK 8, USA 6) circular needles, 80 cm (32 in) in length from tip to tip
* Darning needle
* Scissors

METHOD

Knitted in the round from the top down.

Cosy

Upper body

With 4 mm (UK 8, USA 6) circular needles and Noro Silk Garden Lite, refer to Method 2, The Holy Cast-On (see page 10) to cast on 8 stitches.

Rnd 1 (and each alternate round): Knit.
Rnd 2: Increase once in every stitch (by knitting into the front and back of it) to end of round (16 sts).
Rnd 4: *K1, increase once in next stitch, repeat from * to end of round (24 sts).
Rnd 6: *K2, increase once in next stitch, repeat from * to end of round (32 sts).
Rnd 8: *K3, increase once in next stitch, repeat from * to end of round (40 sts).
Rnd 10: *K4, increase in next stitch, repeat from * to end of round (48 sts).

Continue in this increasing pattern until there are 10 stitches in each segment of the pie (80 sts in total).

Sides

Up to this point you have been working round and round. Now, you are going to work BACK and FORTH in ROWS. However, start working the Sides by knitting the first half of the next ROUND in the following pattern (Row 1). When you have completed the half round, turn the work so that you are purling across the stitches you have just made (Row 2).

Ball the wool into its many colours to work the Graph pattern (opposite). Colour One (C1) is the one already on the needles; Colour Two (C2) is the new colour you introduce, and so on for C3, C4, C5, C6, C7.

Row 1: *K2 (C1), K2 (C2), repeat from * to end of row.
Row 2: *P2 (C2), P2 (C1), repeat from * to end row.
Row 3: *K2 (C2), K2 (C3), repeat from * to end of row.
Row 4: *P2 (C3), P2 (C2), repeat from * to end of row.

Now follow the chequerboard pattern on the Graph as it is written or until the Sides measure just below the spout and handle of your teapot.

Lower ribbing

Now choose one colour to rib to the bottom hem (see Note below before you begin).

Note. For a smooth colour change at this point, you want to purl across the SAME colour as the row before and knit across the CONTRASTING colour of the row before.

Row 1: *K2, P2, repeat from * to end of row.
Row 2: *K2, P2, repeat from * to end of row.

Repeat these 2 rows twice more (6 rows in total).

Cast off loosely.

Work the second Side the same. I matched the colours closely to the first Side.

Chequerboard pattern for Sides

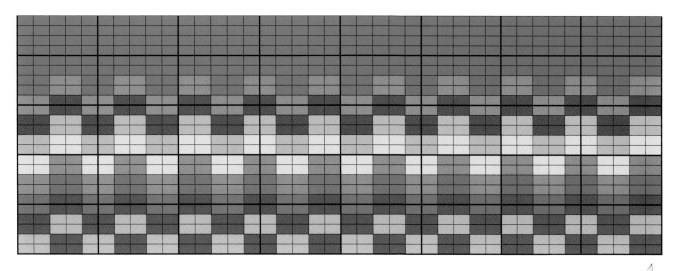

Start here once the Upper Body is knitted

Fez

With 4 mm (UK 8, USA 6) circular needles and Noro Silk Garden Lite, work as for the Upper Body, working the increasing pattern until there are 9 stitches in each segment of the pie (72 stitches in total).

Work the rim in garter stitch as follows:
Rnd 1: Purl.
Rnd 2: Knit.

Repeat these 2 rounds 7 more times (16 rounds in total).

Work the inside hem in stocking stitch, as follows:
Rnds 17–30: Knit.

Cast off loosely.

Lining

Yes, make a Lining, but make it after you have completed all the other parts, including weaving the rim of the Fez. Then, with whatever colours you have left, use 4 mm (UK 8, USA 6) circular needles and Noro Silk Garden Lite yarn to make Basic Tea Cosy No 1 (see page 20).

Putting it all together

Sew the sides of the Base together below the spout and handle, using mattress stitch (see page 16). Turn the Lining inside out and insert into the outer cosy. Sew together around the spout and handle openings only.

Cut the stiff interfacing to size to fit the Fez. You need a circle crown and a straight rim interfacing. I used a plate of a similar size to mark out a circle and a ruler to measure the depth and length of the straight rim. Everyone's Fez will be a little different, depending on the yarn you use and your tension.

Insert the circle interfacing into the crown of the Fez and the straight interfacing into the rim. Turn the stocking stitch hem up inside the rim. Using a darning needle and the same coloured yarn as the Fez crown edge, sew the hem into place taking care to hide the stitches in the knitting.

Weaving the rim

Choose three yummy colours to weave into the rim of the Fez, then do a little Wonder Weaving (see page 16). The instructions for how to do the Wonder Weave say

to tie the threads off at the back of the fabric, but you will be working on a finished Fez, all stiffened and sewn up already. To start the new thread, bring the needle across and under the work from about 5 cm (2 in) away from the point you need it. It will stay there without tying it to anything. Cut the end yarn at the place of entry, right up close to the fabric.

Tassel

You know how to make a tassel, don't you?! Wrap a bit of yarn around your fingers (Step 1), tie it together at one end (Step 2), cut the other end, go back to the tied end and wrap and tie again. See the finished tea cosy picture? Like that.

Step 1

Step 2

Daisy Daisy
(sung to the bicycle song)

Recognise them? YES, they are the leaves from Lily of the Valley in
How Tea Cosies Changed the World. Rearranged. Magnificently, don't
you think, into something altogether different. Ah! Ideas! The more ideas
you have, the more ideas you have.

FOR SUE OF ADELAIDE

SIZE

To fit a six-cup teapot that stands 13 cm (5 in) tall (not
including the knob) and 15 cm (6 in) in diameter (not
including the spout and handle). Choose a large round
teapot with a flat top, preferably with the lid knob
sitting flush (not poking up). The flower will sit down
flat with the petals spreading wide. It isn't absoLUTEly
necessary but it will look SOOOOO much better. Looks
are important. Yes they are.

MATERIALS

* 3 x 50 g (1¾ oz) balls Noro Kureyon yarn – Petals
* 1 x 50 g (1¾ oz) ball of any sturdy 8-ply (DK) yarn
  to coordinate with Petals – Lining
* A little bit of Orange mohair, enough to make half a
  pompom

EQUIPMENT

* One set 5 mm (UK 6, USA 8) circular needles, 80 cm
  (32 in) from tip to tip – Petals
* 4 mm (UK 8, USA 6) circular needles – Lining
* Pompom maker
* Scissors
* Darning needle

METHOD

The Petals are knitted in the round from the centre out.

The Lining is knitted in the round from the top down.

Cosy

Petals (make 8)

With 5 mm (UK 6, USA 8) circular needles and Noro Kureyon yarn, cast on 12 (+ 1) stitches and join in the round using Method 1 (see page 9).

Rnds 1 & 2: (K5, P1) twice.
Rnd 3: (K2, M1, <u>K1</u>, M1, K2, P1) twice (16 sts).

Note. The underlined <u>K1</u> forms the centre vein of the Petal and helps with each reading too. Helpful aren't I?

For the increasing pattern work as follows:
Rnds 4 & 5: (K7, P1) twice.
Rnd 6: (K3, M1, <u>K1</u>, M1, K3, P1) twice (20 sts).
Rnds 7 & 8: (K9, P1) twice.
Rnd 9: (K4, M1, <u>K1</u>, M1, K4, P1) twice (24 sts).
Rnds 10 & 11: (K11, P1) twice.
Rnd 12: (K5, M1, <u>K1</u>, M1, K5, P1) twice (28 sts).
Rnds 13 & 14: (K13, P1) twice.
Rnd 15: (K6, M1, <u>K1</u>, M1, K6, P1) twice (32 sts).
Rnds 16 & 17: (K15, P1) twice.
Rnd 18: (K7, M1, <u>K1</u>, M1, K7, P1) twice (36 sts).
Rnds 19–22: (K17, P1) twice.

For the decreasing pattern, work as follows:
Rnd 23: (K6, ssk, <u>K1</u>, K2tog, K6, P1) twice (32 sts).
Rnds 24–26: (K15, P1) twice.
Rnd 27: (K5, ssk, <u>K1</u>, K2tog, K5, P1) twice (28 sts).
Rnds 28–30: (K13, P1) twice.
Rnd 31: (K4, ssk, <u>K1</u>, K2tog, K4, P1) twice (24 sts).
Rnds 32–34: (K11, P1) twice.
Rnd 35: (K3, ssk, <u>K1</u>, K2tog, K3, P1) twice (20 sts).
Rnds 36–38: (K9, P1) twice.
Rnd 39: (K2, ssk, <u>K1</u>, K2tog, K2, P1) twice (16 sts).

Rnds 40–42: (K7, P1) twice.
Rnd 43: (K1, ssk, <u>K1</u>, K2tog, K1, P1) twice (12 sts).

Now it changes a little bit:
Rnds 44 & 45: (K5, P1) twice.
Rnd 46: (Ssk, <u>K1</u>, K2tog, P1) twice (8 sts).
Rnd 47: (K3, P1) twice.
Rnd 48: Ssk, K2tog, ssk, K2tog (4 sts).

Cut a long piece of yarn and draw it up through the remaining 4 stitches to a nice point. Line the veins up on either side of the Petal and, with your needle and thread, sew the back and front together down the centre vein.

Lining

YES. Absolutely you need a Lining. Use the Basic Tea Cosy No 1 (see page 20), with 4 mm (UK 8, USA 6) circular needles and any sturdy 8-ply (DK) yarn of similar hue to the yarn you used for the Petals.

Central floret

With the little bit of Orange mohair and the pompom maker, make half a pompom. Oh OK, so how does one make HALF a pompom? Wrap half the circumference of the pompom maker. Be very careful when you cut between the two halves of the pompom maker. Best to have it sitting all on a table so that you can gently work the tying yarn between the two parts without losing all the cut pompom threads.

Putting it all together

Overlap the Petals at their centre point (the fat ends) to make a flower, and pin them in place, making the centre hole as small as possible. Try it on the flat-top teapot and, when you are happy with the way it is sitting, sew together along the Petals out towards their tips, but not so they are joined at the Petal edges. Tie the Central Floret (half pompom) in the centre. Put the Lining on the teapot and the flower on the Lining, with the Petals lined up so that the spout and handle poke through happily. Stitch the flower to the Lining around the central top only.

Tibetan Tea Warriors

Knit three or you'll have a war on your hands.

FOR ALL THE WONDERFUL WORKSHOP WOMEN

SIZE

To fit a four-cup teapot that stands 11 cm (4¼ in) tall (not including the knob) and 14 cm (5½ in) in diameter (not including the spout and handle).

MATERIALS

* 1 x 50 g (1¾ oz) ball Noro Silk Garden Lite yarn, Main Colour (MC) (see Note)
* 1 x 100 g (3½ oz) ball Cascade 220 yarn, Contrast Colour (CC) (see Another note)
* Felted balls and wooden beads (optional)
* Polyester fibrefill

EQUIPMENT

* One set 4.5 mm (UK 7, USA 7) circular needles, 80 cm (32 in) from tip to tip
* Darning needle
* Pompom maker

METHOD

Knitted in the round from the top down.

Note. Noro comes in all sorts of beautiful colours, as does the Cascade. Choose what you love best. Be game. Have fun with the colour.

Another note. Cascade 220 only comes in 100 g (3½ oz) skeins, so you'll get a couple of tea cosies out of that lot of wool. If you prefer to buy less, choose one 50 g (1¾ oz) ball of any sturdy 8-ply (DK) yarn.

Body

Crown

With 4.5 mm (UK 7, USA 7) circular needles and MC (Noro) yarn, refer to Method 2, The Holy Cast-On (see page 10) to cast on 8 stitches.

Rnd 1: Knit.
Rnd 2: Increase once in every stitch (by knitting into the front and back of it) to end of round (16 sts).
Rnds 3 & 4: Knit.
Rnd 5: *K1, increase once in next stitch, repeat from * to end of round (24 sts).
Rnds 6 & 7: Knit.
Rnd 8: *K2, increase once in next stitch, repeat from * to end of round (32 sts).
Rnds 9 & 10: Knit.
Rnd 11: *K3, increase once in next stitch, repeat from * to end of round (40 sts).
Rnds 12 & 13: Knit.
Rnd 14: *K4, increase once in next stitch, repeat from * to end of round (48 sts).
Rnds 15 & 16: Knit.
Rnd 17: *K5, increase once in next stitch, repeat from * to end of round (56 sts).
Rnd 18: Knit.

Rim

Rnd 1: Purl.
Rnd 2: Knit.
Join in the CC (Cascade) yarn. Leave the MC yarn attached to pick up again later. Twist the two colours (once only) at the beginning of each alternate round to take the waiting colour with you on the way down to where it is needed again.

Rnd 3: Loop stitch every stitch in the round.
Rnd 4: Purl.
Rnd 5: Loop stitch every stitch in the round.
Rnd 6: Purl.

What is the Loop Stitch I hear you ask? (See page 14.)

Upper body

Rnd 1: Using MC (Noro), knit to end of round.
Rnd 2: *K5, K2tog, repeat from * to end of round (48 sts).
Rnd 3: Knit.

Time to choose your warrior's apparel. Follow the blue-and-green checked and stripy pattern below, or go to the colour Graphs (opposite) for a couple of other wardrobe options.

Rnds 4 & 5: *K2 (MC), K2 (CC), repeat from * to end of round.
Rnds 6 & 7: *K2 (CC), K2 (MC), repeat from * to end of round.
Rnds 8 & 9: *K2 (MC), K2 (CC), repeat from * to end of round.
Continue using MC (Noro) only but carrying CC (Cascade) down with you on the inside.
Rnd 10: Knit.
Rnd 11: *K5, increase once in next stitch, repeat from * to end of round (56 sts).
Rnd 12: Knit.
Rnd 13: Change to CC (Cascade), knit.
Rnds 14–16: Purl.
Rnd 17: Using MC, knit to end of round.
Rnd 18: *K6, increase once in next stitch, repeat from * to end of round (64 sts).
Rnd 19: Knit.

Tibetan Tea Warriors Upper Body and Side variations

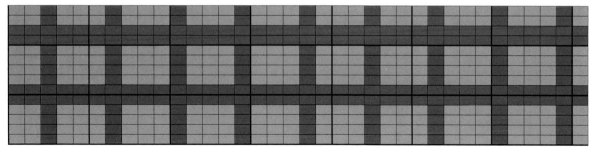

36 stitches on each Side of Cosy Bowl

This graph pattern is one round fewer than the number of WRITTEN rounds. Don't worry – just continue working from Rnd 10.

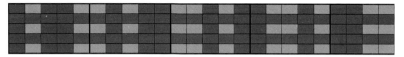

24 stitches each Side of Upper Body

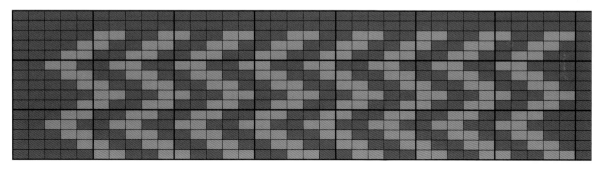

36 stitches on each Side of Cosy Bowl

This graph pattern is one round more than the number of WRITTEN rounds. Don't worry – just continue working from Rnd 10.

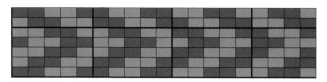

24 stitches each Side of Upper Body

Very important note. It is imperative that you now measure the cosy against your teapot. You may need more than 64 stitches in the round to cover your pot. If you do, *K7, increase once in next stitch, repeat from * to end of round (72 sts). Measure again. If you need to increase again, knit one round, and then, in next round *K8, increase once in next stitch, repeat from * to end of round (80 sts).

Sides
Worked in ROWS (not rounds).

Find the point where the working yarn is. This becomes the first stitch of the first ROW on one SIDE of the cosy. Up to this point, you have been working round and round. Now you are going to work BACK and FORTH on half the stitches only.

Because you are now working in ROWS, and working back across the stitches you have just made (not onto the next stitch in the round), you will have the reverse (WRONG) side of the knitting facing you.

Each Side of the cosy will have 32 stitches (or 36 sts, or 40 sts). Work pattern as follows, or go back to the graphed variations.

Row 1 (wrong side): *P2 (CC), P2 (MC), repeat from * to end of row.
Row 2 (right side): *K2 (MC), K2 (CC), repeat from * to end of row.
Repeat these 2 rows 4 more times (10 rows in total).

Tip. Twist the colours around each other once at the beginning of every row.

Measure the Side length against your teapot. Continue working until the Sides measure to the point just below the handle and spout. Cut the yarn leaving a long thread to darn in later. Move these stitches onto the flexible cable of the circular needles and ignore them while you work the other Side.

Make Side 2 as for Side 1.

Rolled hem
Join in the round using Method 3 (see page 12).

It is time to discard the MC (Noro) wool and continue in CC (Cascade) only.

Rnds 1–10: Knit.
Cast off.

Lining

Yes, make a Lining. With 4.5 mm (UK 7, USA 7) circular needles and Cascade yarn, knit the Basic Tea Cosy No 1 (see page 20).

Top knots

You could make pompoms to do the job. The best pompoms have a lot of wool so don't be stingy with the wrapping around your pompom maker. Use two threads to tie around the middle so that it doesn't break in the making. No pompom comes off the pompom maker in perfect shape so get out your sharpest scissors and practise your topiary skills.

But I used felted balls that I bought from a shop, and wooden beads I've had in my cupboard a long time. I wrapped a bit of yarn around my fingers and tied it together and pulled that tie down through the wooden bead and felted ball and through the top of the tea cosy right down to the inside of the lining.

Feathers might look pretty damn good too. Make it up. Remember! Smoke and mirrors. Costume design. It's all yours to play with.

Putting it all together

Fill the top with not too much and not too little fibrefill, spreading it into the corners of the tower top. Tighten the loopy fringe by holding onto the Rim and easing the loops out and away from the cosy. Do it row by row. The loops will tighten up nicely and stay more secure. Then, if you like, cut the loop ends to give a Cut Loop End effect.

Turn the Lining inside out and place into the outer cosy. With darning needle and matching wool, sew the inner and outer cosies together with a simple tacking stitch around the spout and handle openings.

Sew on your magnificent pompom or top knot.

Ms Daffy Dill

You might recognise Ms Dill. She has previously shown off as Australia's Official Biggest Morning Tea Daffodil Tea Cosy. Now, unofficially official, she reappears here as herself, plain old Daffy, but still doing the work of ambassador, whenever and wherever she is needed, to help raise funds for the Cancer Council. Knit her, love her, raffle her, for all our sisters.

FOR VICKY AND HER SISTER SUSAN
AND FOR ROSIE AND HER SISTER RHONDA

SIZE

To fit a four-cup teapot that stands 11 cm (4¼ in) tall (not including the knob) and 14 cm (5½ in) in diameter (not including the spout and handle).

MATERIALS

* 2 x 50 g (1¾ oz) balls Jo Sharp Classic DK yarn: Colour 357 (China)
* 1 x 50 g (1¾ oz) ball 8-ply (DK) yarn: Daffodil Yellow (see Note)
* 30 cm (12 in) square very stiff non-woven interfacing
* Handful of polyester fibrefill

EQUIPMENT

* One set 4 mm (UK 8, USA 6) circular needles, 80 cm (32 in) from tip to tip
* 4 mm (UK 8, USA G/6) crochet hook – Daffodil Stamen

METHOD

Knitted in the round from the top down.

Note. I wish you the best in your search for a beautiful sunny yellow. Mine is a cotton yarn I bought in France. I've not been able to find anything quite like the colour again and can't bring myself to use anything else, even for Your Fabulousnesses, wot bought One's book and want to make same.

Body
Tall pointy base

With 4 mm (UK 8, USA 6) circular needles and Jo Sharp Classic DK wool (China), refer to Method 2, The Holy Cast-On (see page 10) to cast on 8 stitches.

Rnd 1: Knit.
Rnd 2: Increase once in every stitch (by knitting into the front and back of it) to end of round (16 sts).
Rnds 3–7: Knit.
Rnd 8: *K1, increase once in next stitch, repeat from * to end of round (24 sts).
Rnds 9–13: Knit.
Rnd 14: *K2, increase once in next stitch, repeat from * to end of round (32 sts).
Rnds 15–19: Knit.
Rnd 20: *K3, increase once in next stitch, repeat from * to end of round (40 sts).
Rnds 21–25: Knit.
Rnd 26: *K4, increase once in next stitch, repeat from * to end of round (48 sts).
Rnds 27–31: Knit.
Rnd 32: *K5, increase once in next stitch, repeat from * to end of round (56 sts).
Rnds 33–37: Knit.
Rnd 38: *K6, increase once in next stitch, repeat from * to end of round (64 sts).
Rnds 39–43: Knit.
Rnd 44: *K7, increase once in next stitch, repeat from * to end of round (72 sts).
Measure against your teapot. If the circumference is now big enough, go to the next bit, if not, continue in the same increasing pattern until it is.
Rnd 45: Knit.

Sides

Up to this point you have been working round and round. Now you are going to work BACK and FORTH in ROWS. Find the point where the working yarn is. This becomes the first stitch of the first ROW on ONE SIDE of the cosy. You will have the wrong side of stocking stitch facing you.

Row 1: K1, P1, place marker (pm), purl to the last 2 sts, K1, P1.
Row 2: (K1, P1) twice, K1, pm, knit to 1 st before marker, P1, remove marker (rm), K1, P1.
Row 3: (K1, P1) three times, pm, purl to 1 st before marker, K1, rm, (P1, K1) twice, P1.
Row 4: (K1, P1) four times, K1, pm, knit to 1 st before marker, P1, rm, rib to end of row.
Row 5: (K1, P1) five times, pm, purl to 1 st before marker, K1, rm, rib to end of row.

See how you are creating a ribbed pattern, row by row, in from the edges of the tea cosy sides. It forms a lovely curve, getting from stocking stitch to ribbed stitch and makes a simple base just that much more classy.

Row 6: (K1, P1) six times, K1, pm, knit to 1 st before marker, P1, rm, rib to end of row.
Row 7: (K1, P1) seven times, pm, purl to 1 st before marker, K1, rm, rib to end of row.
Row 8: (K1, P1) eight times, K1, pm, knit to 1 st before marker, P1, rm, rib to end of row.
If you had 72 stitches in the round, 36 stitches on each side, then you will now be up to rib stitch all the way across. If you have more stitches, continue adding an extra rib on the inside edges of the curve on every row.
Row 9: Rib to end of row.

Continue to rib stitch down Side One of the cosy base until it measures all the way to the table. So that means you need to try it on your pot.

Cast off loosely.

Repeat the same instructions for the other Side. Remember, you started with the WRONG SIDE of the tea cosy facing.

Lining
Yes, make a matching lining in Classic DK, using the Basic Tea Cosy No 2 pattern (see page 22).

Daffodil – make 1
Bell
With 4 mm (UK 8, USA 6) circular needles and Yellow yarn, refer to Method 2, The Holy Cast-On (see page 10) to cast on 6 stitches.

Rnd 1: Knit. Place marker to show the beginning of the round.
Rnd 2: Increase once in every stitch (by knitting into the front and back of it) to end of round (12 sts).
Rnd 3: Knit.
Rnd 4: *K3, M1, repeat from * to end of round (16 sts).
Rnds 5–10: Knit.
Rnd 11: *K4, M1, repeat from * to end of round (20 sts).

Rnd 12: Knit.
Rnd 13: K2, *M1, K5, repeat from * to last 3 sts, M1, K3 (24 sts).
Rnds 14 & 15: Knit.

To make picot edging:
Rnd 16: *Yfwd, K2tog, repeat from * to end of round.

𝒩ote. The yfwd creates one large stitch. When you knit into it in the next round, it creates a lace hole.

Rnds 17 & 18: Knit.
Rnd 19: *K4, K2tog, repeat from * to end of round (20 sts).
Rnd 20: Knit.
Rnd 21: K1, K2tog, *K3, K2tog, repeat from * to last 2 sts, K2 (16 sts).
Rnds 22–26: Knit.
Rnd 27: *K2, K2tog, repeat from * to end of round (12 sts).
Rnd 28: Knit.
Rnd 29: *K2tog, repeat from * to end of round (6 sts). Instead of casting off, thread the end through a darning needle and through the last 6 stitches. Pull up tight to close the hole and sew a couple of holding stitches. Fold the Bell in on itself, along the picot edging, with the smaller section down inside the larger section. Pull through the remaining wool to use later when putting the daffodil together.

Petals (make 6)

With 4 mm (UK 8, USA 6) circular needles and Yellow yarn, cast on 12 (+ 1) stitches and join in the round, using Method 1 (see page 9). You will be working from the bottom up.

Rnd 1: (K5, P1) twice.
Rnd 2: (K2, M1, K1, M1, K2, P1) twice (16 sts).
Rnd 3: (K7, P1) twice.
Rnd 4: (K3, M1, K1, M1, K3, P1) twice (20 sts).
Rnd 5: (K9, P1) twice.
Rnd 6: (K4, M1, K1, M1, K4, P1) twice (24 sts).
Rnd 7: (K11, P1) twice.
Rnd 8: (Ssk, K3, M1, K1, M1, K3, K2tog, P1) twice (24 sts).
Rnd 9: (K11, P1) twice.
Rnd 10: (Ssk, K3, M1, K1, M1, K3, K2tog, P1) twice (24 sts).
Rnd 11: (K11, P1) twice.
Rnd 12: (Ssk, K7, K2tog, P1) twice (20 sts).
Rnds 13 & 14: (K9, P1) twice.
Rnd 15: (Ssk, K5, K2tog, P1) twice (16 sts).
Rnds 16 & 17: (K7, P1) twice.
Rnd 18: (Ssk, K3, K2tog, P1) twice (12 sts).
Rnds 19 & 20: (K5, P1) twice.
Rnd 21: (Ssk, K1, K2tog, P1) twice (8 sts).
Rnd 22: (K3, P1) twice.

Thread the yarn end through a darning needle and through the last 8 stitches. Close the loop but not too tightly yet. Thread the yarn through again, but this time omitting stitch numbers 4 and 8. They were your purl stitches. Now you can pull the yarn tight. This will help make a neat Petal tip. The purl stitches form the folds at the sides of the Petal. Line up the front and back of the Petal and sew some hidden stitches down through the centre to hold it in place.

Stamen (make 3)

Using a 4 mm (UK 8, USA G/6) crochet hook, make 6 chain.

1 htr into 2nd ch from hook, 1 slip st into each ch to the bottom of the stamen. Fasten off.

Putting the flower together

Place one Petal on top of another, so that they overlap from centre to centre, and repeat until all the petals are in place. Sew together, hiding your sewing stitches by following the line of your knit stitches. The overlapping will help the Petals to sit upright when you finally bring the sixth and first Petals together. Sew the Stamens into the Bell, then sew the Bell in the centre of the Petals.

Putting it all together

Draw a circle within the 30 cm (12 in) square of stiff interfacing and cut it out. Draw a line from the circumference to the centre and cut along it. Then wrap the interfacing around itself to form a cone to fit inside the Tall Pointy Base. Trim around the bottom edge so that it doesn't poke out at the spout and handle openings. Put a little handful of fibrefill into the cone, not to fill it up, not to give it shape, just to help the interfacing do its job well.

When you are happy with the fit, turn the Lining inside out and place up into the Tall Pointy Base. With darning needle and China blue wool, sew the inner and outer cosies together around the spout and handle openings.

Stitch the Daffodil to the top of the Tall Pointy Base.

Jester Cuppa Tea

This tea cosy belongs to Marilyn Banfield. She was a student in my class at the 2013 Sturt Winter School, held every year in Mittagong, NSW. I love it when students embrace the design component of the class without any regard for their abilities and with every expectation that they will be able to turn a scratchy drawing into a sensational knitted thing. Marilyn stretched my interpretive skills to the limit and together we came up with Jester Cuppa.

FOR MARILYN OF SYDNEY

SIZE

To fit a four-cup teapot that stands 11 cm (4¼ in) tall (not including the knob) and 14 cm (5½ in) in diameter (not including the spout and handle).

MATERIALS

* Cascade 220 yarn (see Note)
* 2 x 50 g (1¾ oz) balls Noro Silk Garden Lite
* Polyester fibrefill

Note. This is a terrific pattern to use up the odd balls in your stash, because each of the Jester Peaks can be in different colours, and the Base can be different again. 100 g (3½ oz) of any sturdy 8-ply (DK) yarn in plain colours will do and, for the diamond pattern, 100 g (3½ oz) of any 8-ply (DK) variegated yarn. I used 2 x 50 g (1¾ oz) balls Noro Silk Garden Lite and 5 different colours of Cascade 220 (which only comes in 100 g skeins).

EQUIPMENT

* One set 5 mm (UK 6, USA 8) circular needles, 80 cm (32 in) from tip to tip – Peaks and Little Triangles
* One set 5 mm (UK 6, USA 8) circular needles, 100 cm (40 in) from tip to tip – Base
* Darning needle
* Scissors
* Pompom makers

METHOD

The Jester Peaks are knitted in the round from the top down. Each Side of the Base is knitted separately and in the round, forming an Outer and a Lining all at once.

Each segment of the cosy (3 Jester Peaks and Base) is made with two colours. Choose a plain colour (referred to as MC or Main Colour) and a variegated colour (referred to as CC or Contrasting Colour) for each segment.

Jester peaks – make 3

With 5 mm (UK 6, USA 8), 80 cm (32 in) circular needles and MC, refer to Method 2, The Holy Cast-On (see page 10) to cast on 6 stitches.

If you are happy reading a Graph, go straight to the Graph (opposite).

If you'd like a bit of help getting started, then here it is – before you go off to the Graph.

Rnd 1: Knit.

Note. There are two ways to make an extra stitch in this pattern (see page 15): M1 (make 1); the other is 'Increase' which means to knit into the front and back of the next stitch before moving it over to your working needle.

Rnd 2: Increase once in every stitch to end of round (12 sts).
Rnds 3 & 4: Knit.

Rnd 5: *K2, M1, repeat from * to end of round (18 sts).
Rnds 6–8: Knit.
Rnd 9: K2(MC), *K1(CC), K5(MC), repeat from * once more, K1(CC), K3(MC).
Rnd 10: K1(MC), *K3(CC), K3(MC), repeat from * once more, K3(CC), K2(MC).
Rnd 11: K1(MC), *{increase once in next stitch, K1, increase once in next stitch}(CC), K3(MC), repeat from * once more, {increase once in next stitch, K1, increase once in next stitch}(CC), K2(MC) (24 sts).
Rnd 12: *K3(CC), K1(MC), repeat from * to end of round.

That's it. You are on your own. Off you go to the Graph. Start where it says HERE!

Note. When you get to the last 7 rounds of using the two colours, be sure to weave in the travelling yarn loosely at the back of the work as you go – every 3rd or 4th stitch.

Break off CC and knit the last rounds of the Graph in MC before loosely casting off.

Jester Peaks

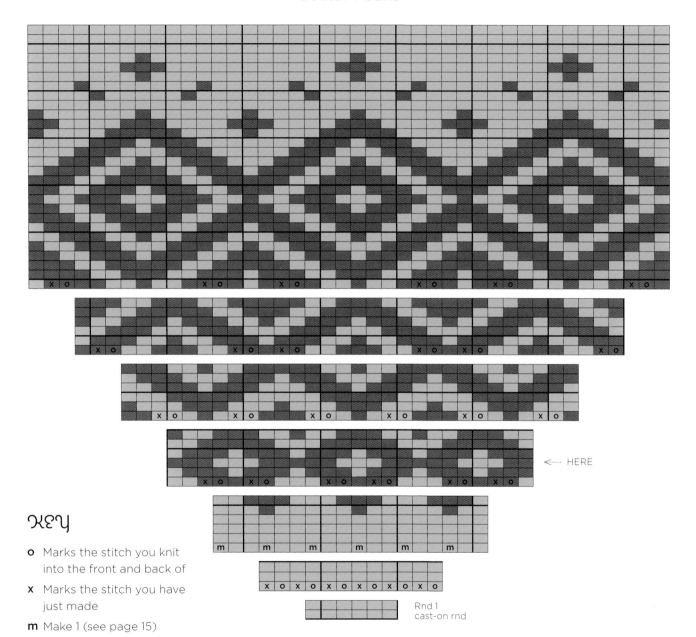

←---- HERE

KEY

o Marks the stitch you knit into the front and back of

x Marks the stitch you have just made

m Make 1 (see page 15)

Rnd 1
cast-on rnd

Base A

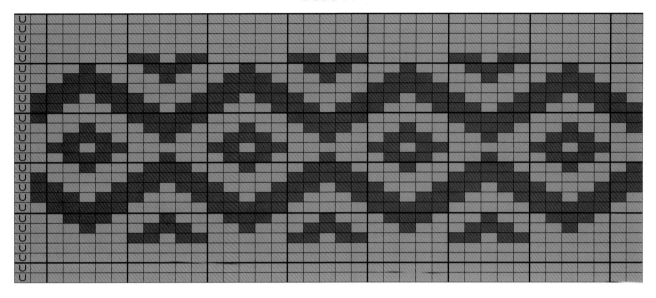

U marks the purl stitch at the end of each half round

Base B

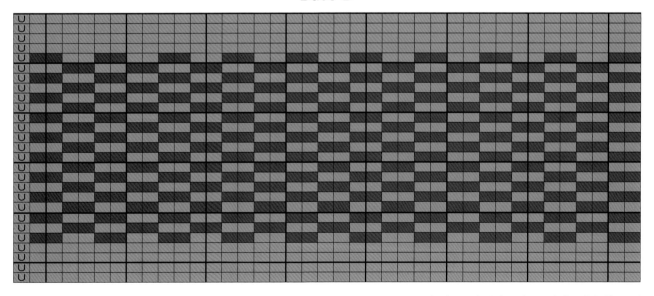

U marks the purl stitch at the end of each half round

Base

Little triangles

Make 3 for Side One of the Base.

With 5 mm (UK 6, USA 8), 80 cm (32 in) circular needles and MC, refer to Method 2, The Holy Cast-On (see page 10) to cast on 8 stitches.

Rnd 1: (K3, P1) twice.
Rnd 2: (K1, M1, K1, M1, K1, P1) twice (12 sts).

Note. The underlined K1 indicates the centre stitch of the triangle. The purled stitch at the end of each half creates a nice crease or fold in the knitting.

Rnd 3: (K5, P1) twice.
Rnd 4: (K2, M1, K1, M1, K2, P1) twice (16 sts).
Rnd 5: (K7, P1) twice.
Rnd 6: (K3, M1, K1, M1, K3, P1) twice (20 sts).
Rnd 7: (K9, P1) twice.
Rnd 8: (K4, M1, K1, M1, K4, P1) twice (24 sts).
Rnd 9: (K11, P1) twice.
Rnd 10 (this is a little different): (K5, M1, K6, P1) twice (26 sts).
Rnd 11: Knit.

Do not cast off. Break the yarn, leaving a long thread to darn in later. Place the stitches onto the longer – 100 cm (40 in) – set of circular needles to wait patiently while you knit up the next Little Triangle.

When all three Little Triangles are sitting on the longer needles, take a moment to tie them together where they sit side by side, on the inside, with a small piece of yarn the same colour. Tie off and secure the cut threads as well.

You are now ready to knit in the round again, joining the three Little Triangles together at the same time. There is now a total of 78 stitches, 39 stitches for the outer and 39 stitches for the lining.

Side One Outer: Knit Graph Base A pattern for 38 stitches. Purl the 39th stitch.
Side One Lining: Knit Graph Base B pattern for 38 stitches. Purl the 39th stitch.

The purled stitch at the end of each half creates a nice crease or fold in the knitting.

Follow Graphs A and B (opposite) alternately as you work the Side Outer and then the Side Lining.

After knitting the last four rounds of the Graphs, set up the needles, as in the photo (below), ready to work the Little Triangles at the top. Use a marker to hold the front and back together while you work the first Little Triangle.

Rnd 1: (K12, P1) twice (26 sts).
Rnd 2: (K4, ssk, K6, P1) twice. Yes, only decrease once, front and back, to bring the triangle to an even number of stitches (24 sts).
Rnd 3: (K11, P1) twice.
Rnd 4: (K3, ssk, <u>K1</u>, K2tog, K3, P1) twice (20 sts).
Rnd 5: (K9, P1) twice.
Rnd 6: (K2, ssk, <u>K1</u>, K2tog, K2, P1) twice (16 sts).
Rnd 7: (K7, P1) twice.
Rnd 8: (K1, ssk, <u>K1</u>, K2tog, K1, P1) twice (12 sts).
Rnd 9: (K5, P1) twice.
Rnd 10: (Ssk, <u>K1</u>, K2tog, P1) twice (8 sts).
Rnd 11: (Ssk, K2tog) twice. Yes, without a knit round in between decrease rounds.

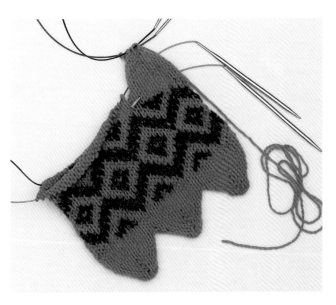

Cut a long thread and, with a darning needle, draw up through the remaining 4 stitches and secure with a couple of tidy stitches.

Set up the needles again for the next 26 stitches – 13 front and 13 back and knit the next Little Triangle. Ditto the third Little Triangle.

Circle tray

The Circle Tray will work as an inside base to the Jester Peaks and hold the whole tea cosy together.

With 5 mm (UK 6, USA 8) needles and Cascade yarn, refer to Method 2, The Holy Cast-On (see page 10) to cast on 8 stitches.

Work the increasing pattern for the Upper Body of the Basic Tea Cosy No 1 (see page 20) until you have a total of 80 stitches.

Cast off.

Pompoms

Make three magnificent little ones.

Putting it all together

To block or not to block

BLOCK! Which simply means to wet everything thoroughly through before sewing it together. Squeeze all the water out of each piece and spread out to dry. Make some cardboard cones for the Jester Peaks to dry on.

When everything is dry and sitting nicely, insert a little bit of fibrefill into the bottom half of each of the Jester Peaks. They need to sit up a little bit and then fall over at their halfway point. Play with this until you are happy, then sew them to each other, as per the diagram (below), and then to the Circle Tray.

Sew the Base sides together above and below the handle and spout openings. Sew the Circle Tray, with its Jester Peaks already in place, to the cosy Base, lining it all up just below the top Little Triangles.

And last, but not least, sew on the three little pompoms for a final fabulous finish.

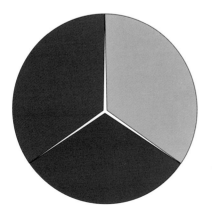

Diagram for sewing the Jester Peaks together.

Russian Caravan

Nerdy Knitter Test: give a left-handed knitter – a true mirror-image, left-handed knitter – a right-to-left colour graph to read, with left needle to right needle text instructions, to test a downwardly spiralling pattern. Lost? Pamela wasn't. Pamela worked Russian Caravan, correcting mistakes, making suggestions and knitting up a perfectly handsome fellow. Thank goodness for Nerdy Knitters, I say. They deserve their capital letters.

FOR PAMELA OF SYDNEY

SIZE

To fit a four-cup teapot that stands 11 cm (4¼ in) tall (not including the knob) and 14 cm (5½ in) in diameter (not including the spout and handle).

MATERIALS

* 1 x 50 g (1¾ oz) ball Brooklyn Tweed Shelter, Main Colour (MC): 25 (Sap) (any Aran DK yarn will do the job nicely) – Cosy
* 1 x 50 g (1¾ oz) ball of any sturdy 8-ply (DK) yarn, Contrast Colour (CC): Purple – Cosy (see Note)
* 1 x 25 g (⅞ oz) ball fine Kid Mohair: Green (to match MC) – Loopy Flower (I used Rowan Kidsilk Haze, 597 (Jelly))
* Small amount of 4-ply yarn, enough to knit a little cylinder about 3 cm (1¼ in) long, doesn't matter what colour – Loopy Flower
* Polyester fibrefill

Note. I used Cascade 220, Colour 8901 (Groseille) which is Purple, and which only comes in 100 g (3½ oz) skeins.

EQUIPMENT

* One set 5 mm (UK 6, USA 8) (or 4.5 mm (UK 7, USA 7) if you are a loose knitter) circular needles, 80 cm (32 in) from tip to tip – Cosy
* One set 2.75 mm (UK 12, USA 2) circular needles, 80 cm (32 in) from tip to tip – Loopy Flower
* Darning needle
* Stitch holder (or another set of circular needles for the resting stitches)
* Scissors

METHOD

Knitted in the round from the top down.

Body

Spiral tower

With 5 mm (UK 6, USA 8) circular needles and CC (Purple) yarn, cast on 16 (+ 1) stitches. Join in the round with Method 1 (see page 9) and work using the Magic Loop (see page 12).

Rnds 1–3: Knit.

A very big helping hint. Mark the beginning of the round by tying a little bit of contrasting coloured wool to the knitted fabric.

Join in MC (Sap) and refer to the Graph (opposite). Read the Graph from the bottom right-hand corner. There are 5 stitches (3 (MC) and 2 (CC)) in the first repeating pattern. The extra (16th) stitch will cause the spiral effect as you work the rounds.

The repeating patterns thereafter (of three rounds each) begin with an increasing round. You will increase by knitting into the front and back of the stitch marked with an 'o'. The 'x' marks the new stitch you have just made.

Another helpful hint. You will have travelling yarn at the back of your colour work, as with the Fair Isle technique. Keep your stitches already worked (on the right needle) stretched out nicely as you change colours so that the travelling yarn does not tighten up all those stitches.

OK, for those who freak out at Graphs, here are the first few rounds written out for you. But only the first few, mind. Then get yourself on over to the Graph.

The Spiral Pattern begins (No 1 on the Graph):

Rnd 4: *K3 (MC), K2 (CC), repeat from * to last stitch, K1 (MC).

Rnd 5: K2 (MC), K2 (CC), *K3 (MC), K2 (CC), repeat from * to last 2 stitches, K2 (MC).

Rnd 6: K1 (MC), K2 (CC), *K3 (MC), K2 (CC), repeat from * to last 3 stitches, K3 (MC).

Now GO TO THE GRAPH for the next 5 rounds. It is good practice for you.

This is how the INCREASING pattern begins (No 2 on the Graph):

Rnd 12: K2 (CC), *K2 (MC), increase once in next stitch (MC), K2 (CC), repeat from * to last 4 stitches, K2 (MC), increase once in next stitch (MC), K1 (CC).

Rnd 13: K1 (CC), *K4 (MC), K2 (CC), repeat from * to end of round.

Rnd 14: *K4 (MC), K2 (CC), repeat from * to last stitch, K1 (MC).

Now you've reached the second increasing pattern (No 3 on the Graph):

Rnd 15: K2 (MC), increase once in next stitch (MC), K2 (CC), *K3 (MC), increase once in next stitch (MC), K2 (CC), repeat from * to last 2 stitches, K2 (MC).

Rnd 16: K3 (MC), K2 (CC), *K5 (MC), K2 (CC), repeat from * to last 3 stitches, K3 (MC).

Rnd 17: K2 (MC), K2 (CC), *K5 (MC), K2 (CC), repeat from * to last 4 stitches, K4 (MC).

And now! Back to the Graph for the rest of the Spiral Tower! You can do it!

Russian Caravan Graph

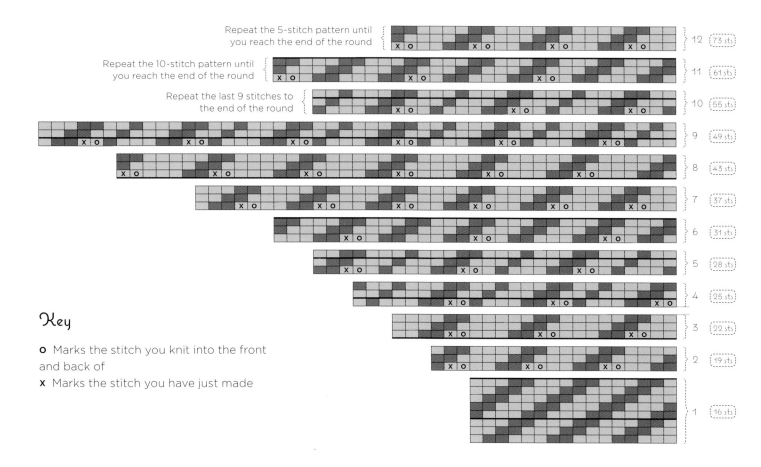

Repeat the 5-stitch pattern until you reach the end of the round — 12 (73 sts)

Repeat the 10-stitch pattern until you reach the end of the round — 11 (61 sts)

Repeat the last 9 stitches to the end of the round — 10 (55 sts)

9 (49 sts)

8 (43 sts)

7 (37 sts)

6 (31 sts)

5 (28 sts)

4 (25 sts)

3 (22 sts)

2 (19 sts)

1 (16 sts)

Key

o Marks the stitch you knit into the front and back of

x Marks the stitch you have just made

REMEMBER, when you are reading your KNITTING, you increase into the MC (Sap) stitch immediately before the two CC (Purple) stitches. When you are reading the GRAPH, the 'o' is the stitch you are knitting into the front and back of, the 'x' is the extra stitch you make.

Sides

Now that you have come to the Sides, which are to be worked in ROWS, leave half the stitches in the centre of the cable and ignore them while you work down the OTHER Side with the needlepoints.

And yes, 73 doesn't divide easily by 2, so put 36 on one side and 37 on the other. All will be well.

Find the point where the working yarn is. This becomes the first stitch of the first ROW on one SIDE of the cosy. Up to this point you have been working round and round. Now you are going to work BACK and FORTH.

Working back across the stitches you have just made, with the WRONG side facing and keeping the spiral pattern correct, purl the first row Knit the second row. Purl the third. Etc, etc, to continue the stocking stitch fabric.

Continue working the spiral pattern. You are so well versed in it now that you can do it in your sleep – and BACK TO FRONT.

When the right side is facing (knitting every stitch), the spiral pattern moves one stitch at a time to the right. When the WRONG side is facing (purling every stitch), the spiral pattern moves one stitch at a time to the left.

Remember to keep those travelling yarns stretched wide across the stitches you make, otherwise there will be no give in the knitted fabric.

Work one Side down to just below your spout and handle. That is about 12 rows on my cosy. It might be more or fewer on your teapot. Measure, measure, measure against the teapot. Finish on a knit row. Cut the yarn, leaving long threads to darn in later. Leave these stitches on the needles. Repeat for the other Side.

When you have the same number of rows on each Side of the tea cosy (COUNT the rows; don't rely on your 'Goodenuff'), cut the MC (Sap) yarn, leaving a long thread to darn in later.

Picot edge hem

With the right side facing and using CC (Purple), JOIN in the ROUND again, using Method 3 (see page 12).

Knit 7 rounds with CC. But wait! You have an uneven number of stitches. K2 together (just the once) in the first round. Voilà – an even number of stitches.

Rnd 8: *Yfwd, K2tog, repeat from * to end of round.
Rnd 9: Knit into every stitch to end of round.

Note. The yfwd becomes one large stitch and, as you knit into it, a lace hole forms.

Rnds 10–16: Knit.
Do NOT cast off.

Lining

Go to Basic Tea Cosy No 3 (see page 24) and work onwards from Continuing the Lining. This will give you a very neat lining attached to the main cosy that will fold up beautifully inside the outer cosy Body.

Picot edge hem around spout and handle openings

This really does finish it off just so, so take the time. WITHOUT the Lining tucked inside and WITH the right side facing – work in the round. Use 5 mm (UK 6, USA 8) circular needles and MC (Sap) to pick up stitches around the spout opening, about 1 stitch per row of knitting. Make sure that you have the same number of stitches (anything from 15 to 20 stitches) on either side of the opening.

Rnds 1 & 2: Knit.
Rnd 3: *Yfwd, K2tog, repeat from * to end of round.
Rnd 4: Knit into every stitch to end of round.
Rnds 5 & 6: Knit.

Cast off loosely.

Loopy flower — make 1

Flower

With 2.75 mm (UK 12, USA 2) circular needles and the little bit of 4-ply, cast on 12 (+ 1) stitches. Join in the round, using Method 1 (see page 9) and work using the Magic Loop (see page 12). Oh, and yes, it is important NOT to use the kid mohair for this little bit. It isn't sturdy enough for holding the bouquet of wool in the centre when putting it all together.

Knit 10 rounds.

Change to Kid Mohair.

Rnd 1: Knit.
Rnd 2: Increase once in every stitch (by knitting into the front and back of it) to end of round (24 sts).
Rnd 3: *Loop1 (see page 14), K1, repeat from * to end of round.
Rnd 4: *K2, increase once in next stitch, repeat from * to end of round (32 sts).
Rnd 5: *Loop3, K1, repeat from * to end of round.
Rnd 6: *K3, increase once in next stitch, repeat from * to end of round (40 sts).
Rnd 7: *Loop4, K1, repeat from * to end of round.
Rnd 8: *K4, increase once in next stitch, repeat from * to end of round (48 sts).
Rnd 9: *Loop5, K1, repeat from * to end of round.
Rnd 10: Knit.
Rnd 11: Loop every stitch.
Rnd 12: *K4, K2tog, repeat from * to end of round (40 sts).
Rnd 13: Knit.

Cast off.

Stigma

Wrap some of the purple Cascade yarn around two fingers. Tie off at one end with a long thread. Cut the other end of the bouquet. Pull the tie down through the centre of the Loopy Flower. Thread the darning needle with the long yarn and sew the bouquet into place in the flower and then sew the completed flower into the top of the Spiral Tower.

Putting it all together

Fill the Spiral Tower with fibrefill, a little bit at a time, not too much, not too little, through the spout and handle openings. It doesn't want to flop, but you want to be able to mould it into shape. Keep filling the Tower down to where the cosy separates to sit over the teapot bowl. Mould and shape. Shape and mould. Try and try again on the teapot. When all is good, push the Lining into the outer cosy. Sew the Lining to the cosy around the spout and handle openings, by turning the Picot Hems to the inside and stitching loosely in place to the Lining.

Desirée

Weellll ... (said in a low growly voice), we didn't know he was a rooster till it was too late and then he would only answer to Desirée.

FOR MY SON BEN, 'COS HE'LL BE ASKING WHERE'S HIS TEA COSY IN THIS BOOK. THERE'S NEVER BEEN ANY DOUBT ABOUT HIM BEING A BOY, BUT.

SIZE

To fit a six-cup teapot that stands 13 cm (5 in) tall (not including the knob) and 15 cm (6 in) in diameter (not including the spout and handle).

It is important to choose a large, round teapot, something with a big belly and a flattish top. Then this well-fed chook will sit low and well on the kitchen table.

MATERIALS

* 1 x 50 g (1¾ oz) ball of any sturdy 8-ply (DK) yarn: Yellow (see Note) – Base, Head/Neck Cone, Rear End Cone
* 2 x 25 g (⅞ oz) ball fine kid mohair: Yellowy-gold – Feathery bits
* A little bit of kid mohair for his Comb and Wattle (Red) and Beak (Orange)
* Very stiff interfacing, about 50 cm (20 in) square
* 2 handfuls polyester fibrefill
* 2 big grey buttons – Eyes
* Glorious rooster feathers for the glorious rooster named Desirée

Note. I used 50 g (1¾ oz) of Cascade 220, Colour 7827 (Goldenrod), which only comes in 100 g (3½ oz) skeins.

EQUIPMENT

* One set 4 mm (UK 8, USA 6) circular needles, 80 cm (32 in) long from tip to tip
* One set 2.75 mm (UK 12, USA 2) circular needles, 80 cm (32 in) long from tip to tip
* Darning needle
* Stitch holder
* Scissors

METHOD

The Base, Head/Neck and Rear End are all knitted in the round, from the top down. The Loopy Feathery sections are knitted in rows. It is essential that you construct first, and feather (with the loopy feathery mohair fabric) last.

Cosy

Base

Make one. With 4 mm (UK 8, USA 6) circular needles and Yellow 8-ply (DK) yarn, make the Basic Tea Cosy No 1 (see page 20).

Head/neck

With 4 mm (UK 8, USA 6) circular needles and Yellow 8-ply yarn, refer to Method 2, The Holy Cast-On (see page 10) to cast on 6 stitches.

Rnd 1: Knit.
Rnd 2: *K1, increase once in next stitch (by knitting into the front and back of it), repeat from * to end of round (9 sts).
Rnd 3: Knit.
Rnd 4: *K2, increase once in next stitch, repeat from * to end of round (12 sts).
Rnd 5: Knit.
Rnd 6: *K3, increase once in next stitch, repeat from * to end of round (15 sts).
Rnd 7: Knit.
Rnd 8: *K4, increase once in next stitch, repeat from * to end of round (18 sts).
Rnd 9: Knit.
Rnd 10: *K5, increase once in next stitch, repeat from * to end of round (21 sts).
Rnd 11: Knit.
Rnd 12: *K6, increase once in next stitch, repeat from * to end of round (24 sts).
Rnds 13 & 14: Knit.

Rearrange the stitches on the magic loop so that they are evenly divided, 12 and 12.
Rnd 15: *K2, increase once in next stitch, repeat from * to end of round (32 sts).
Rnds 16–20: Knit.
Rnd 21: *K3, increase once in next stitch, repeat from * to end of round (40 sts).
Rnds 22–26: Knit.
Rnd 27: *K4, increase once in next stitch, repeat from * to end of round (48 sts).
Rnds 28–32: Knit.
Rnd 33: *K5, increase once in next stitch, repeat from * to end of round (56 sts).
Rnds 34–38: Knit.
Cast off loosely.

Rear end

Work the same as for the Head/Neck, but only as far as the end of **Rnd 26** (40 sts), then cast off loosely.

Putting some of it together

Well, we'll put some of it together now. Sew the Base sides together below the spout and handle openings. With the stiff interfacing, make two cones and insert them into the two knitted cones. Set the whole thing up on your fat round teapot. Sew the cones into place, with the taller Head/Neck cone at the front (poking out over the spout) and the smaller Rear End one leaning towards the handle. They will most likely overlap a bit in the middle. Don't fuss too much about how your construction looks. It will all be covered with the Loopy Feathering.

Desirée **133**

Loopy feathering

If you have never done Loop Stitch (see page 14) before, it might be best to start with feathering Desirée's sides. Even though we are using the same size needles and lighter yarn, Loop Stitch is very holey and stretchy.

Loopy feathery sides (make 2)

With 4 mm (UK 8, USA 6) circular needles and Yellowy-gold kid mohair, cast on 35 stitches. (You are working in ROWS.)

Row 1: Knit.
Row 2: Loop stitch into every stitch. Take your time now. Stop to tighten every stitch by holding the loop in one hand and the knitted fabric in the other and give a little tug. The stitch will close up into a knot, close to the needle.
Repeat the last 2 rows until the feathery fabric reaches from the bottom of the Base side to the place where the cones sit atop.

Cast off loosely.

Loopy feathery rear end

Knitted in ROWS. Yes, I know it's a cone shape, but the sides are seamed together later.

With 4 mm (UK 8, USA 6) circular needles and Yellowy-gold kid mohair, cast on 6 stitches.

Row 1: Knit.
Row 2: *K1, increase once in next stitch (by knitting into the front and back of it), repeat from * to end of row (9 sts).
Row 3: *K1, Loop2, repeat from * to end of row.
Row 4: *K2, increase once in next stitch, repeat from * to end of row (12 sts).
Row 5: *K1, Loop3, repeat from * to end of row.
Row 6: *K3, increase once in next stitch, repeat from * to end of row (15 sts).
Row 7: *K1, Loop4, repeat from * to end of row.
Row 8: *K4, increase once in next stitch, repeat from * to end of row (18 sts).
Row 9: *K1, Loop5, repeat from * to end of row.
Row 10: *K5, increase once in next stitch, repeat from * to end of row (21 sts).
Row 11: *K1, Loop6, repeat from * to end of row.
Row 12: *K6, increase once in next stitch, repeat from * to end of row (24 sts).
Row 13: *K1, Loop7, repeat from * to end of row.
(Try it on the Rear End knitted cone for size. Keep trying it on every few rows for size and follow the pattern until your feather cone fits your knitted cone.)
Row 14: *K2, increase once in next stitch, repeat from * to end of row (32 sts).
Row 15: *K1, Loop3, repeat from * to end of row.
Row 16: *K3, increase once in next stitch, repeat from * to end of row (40 sts).
Row 17: Knit.
Row 18: Loop every stitch.
Row 19: Knit.
Row 20: Loop every stitch.
Row 21: *K4, increase once in next stitch, repeat from * to end of row (48 sts).
Row 22: *K1, Loop5, repeat from * to end of row.
Row 23: Knit.
Cast off loosely.

Loopy feathery head/neck

Knitted in ROWS.

With 4 mm (UK 8, USA 6) circular needles and Yellowy-gold kid mohair, cast on 18 stitches.

Row 1: Knit.
Row 2: *K1, Loop5, repeat from * to end of row.
Row 3: *K5, increase once in next stitch (by knitting into the front and back of it), repeat from * to end of row (21 sts).
Row 4: *K1, Loop6, repeat from * to end of row.
Row 5: *K6, increase once in next stitch, repeat from * to end of row (24 sts).
Row 6: *K1, Loop7, repeat from * to end of row.
Row 7: *K2, increase once in next stitch, repeat from * to end of row (32 sts).
Row 8: *K1, Loop3, repeat from * to end of row.
Row 9: *K3, increase once in next stitch, repeat from * to end of row (40 sts).
Row 10: Knit.
Row 11: Loop every stitch.
Row 12: Knit.
Row 13: Loop every stitch.
(Try it on the Head/Neck knitted cone for size. Keep trying it on every few rows for size and follow the pattern until your feather cone fits your knitted cone.)
Row 14: *K4, increase once in next stitch, repeat from * to end of row (48 sts).
Row 15: *K1, Loop5, repeat from * to end of row.
Row 16: Knit.
Cast off loosely.

Comb — make 2

With 2.75 mm (UK 12, USA 2) circular needles and Red kid mohair, work the Head/Neck pattern to **Rnd 14**.

Rnd 15: Knit.
Cast off loosely.

Beak — make 1

With 2.75 mm (UK 12, USA 2) circular needles and Orange kid mohair, work the Head/Neck pattern to **Rnd 14**.

Rnds 15–17: Knit.
Cast off loosely.

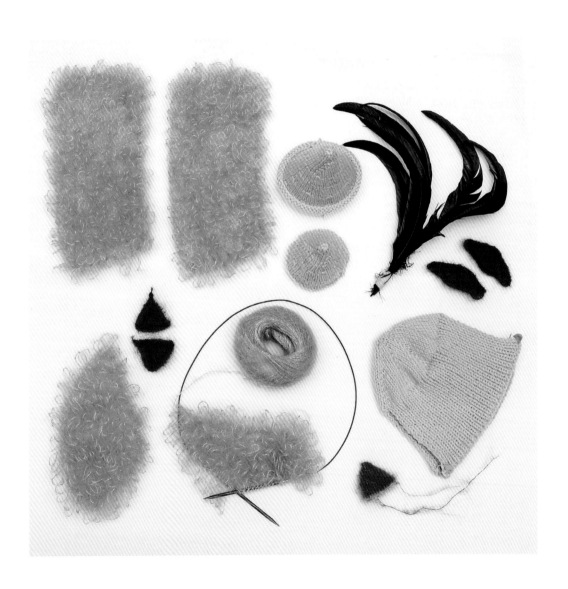

Wattle — make 2

Note. There are two parts to the Wattle, knitted on the straight in ROWS. Now, even though the Wattle is knitted in ROWS, cast on in the ROUND, using Method 2, The Holy Cast-On (see page 10). This Wattle pattern starts from the outer point and works in towards the beak. Casting on this way gives a clean start and sets up the shaping for the Wattle.

With 2.75 mm (UK 12, USA 2) circular needles and Red kid mohair, cast on 7 stitches, using Method 2, The Holy Cast-On. Leave the stitches on the needle (that is, don't move them down onto the flexible cable) and draw up the short yarn of the original loop just a little bit to begin closing these stitches together.

Row 1: Purl. Draw up the short yarn again to close the circle. Continue working in ROWS.
Row 2: K3, M1, K1, M1, K3 (the underlined K1 marks the middle of the work) (9 sts).
Row 3 (and each alternate row): Purl.
Row 4: K4, M1, K1, M1, K4 (11 sts).
Row 6: K5, M1, K1, M1, K5 (13 sts).
Row 8: K6, M1, K1, M1, K6 (15 sts).
Row 10: K2, M1, knit to last 2 stitches, M1, K2 (17 sts).
Row 12: K2, M1, knit to last 2 stitches, M1, K2 (19 sts).
Row 14: K7, ssk, K1, K2tog, K7 (17 sts).
Row 16: K2, ssk, K2, ssk, K1, K2tog, K2, K2tog, K2 (13 sts).
Row 18: K2, ssk, K5, K2tog, K2 (11 sts).
Row 20: K2, ssk, K3, K2tog, K2 (9 sts).
Row 22: K2, ssk, K1, K2tog, K2 (7 sts).
Cast off.

Putting it all together

This is all about sewing. Stretch the orange mohair Beak down over the Head/Neck cone. Stitch it into place around the bottom cast-off edge. Sew the sides of the Loopy Feathery Head/Neck together to form an open-ended cone. Do the same for the Loopy Feathery Rear End. Pull them down over their respective ends on the tea cosy skeleton. Pin the Loopy Feathery Sides onto the Base sides. There will be a bit of stretching and gathering to make them sit nicely. When you are happy, stitch them into place around the edges with a couple of strategically placed stitches in the middle of the Sides.

Stitch the Comb triangle bottom openings together flat. Overlap them a little bit to stitch them into place, just below the orange Beak on the top side of the Head/Neck.

The Wattles are folded in half along the cast-off edges (7 stitches) to enhance their voluptuousness. They will sit side by side just below the Beak on the bottom side of the Head/Neck.

When you are happy with all these wobbly bits, sew on the big grey button Eyes.

Wrap the rooster feathers together tightly at the bottom with some cotton.

With a knitting needle make a hole in the top of the Rear End without breaking the wool. Insert the feathers down into the hole and, with the Yellowy-gold mohair, secure them in place with a couple of stitches.

Cock-a-doodle-doo.

Ranga

Ranga. Ginger. Carrot Top. Bloodnut. Blue.
We are a special mop, err, mob, we are, we are.

FOR ALL THE RANGAS IN THE WORLD

SIZE

To fit a six-cup teapot that stands 13 cm (5 in) tall (not including the knob) and 15 cm (6 in) in diameter (not including the spout and handle).

MATERIALS

* 1 x 50 g (1¾ oz) ball of any sturdy 8-ply (DK) yarn: Orange (see Note)
* 1 x 25 g (⅞ oz) ball fine kid mohair: Orange (I used Rowan Kidsilk Haze, Colour 596 (Marmalade))

Note. I used 50 g (1¾ oz) of Cascade 220, Colour 9542 (Blaze – an Orange colour), which only comes in 100 g (3½ oz) skeins.

EQUIPMENT

* One set 4 mm (UK 8, USA 6) circular needles, 80 cm (32 in) from tip to tip
* Darning needle
* Stitch holder (or another set of circular needles for the resting stitches)
* Scissors

METHOD

Loopy cosy is knitted in the round from the top down.

LOOP STITCH

You will need this (see page 14).

Lining

It is very important to knit the Lining first.

With 4 mm (UK 8, USA 6) circular needles and Orange 8-ply (DK) yarn, make the Basic Tea Cosy No 1 (see page 20). Place the Lining on your teapot. Then you can measure the Loopy Cosy over the Lining as you go.

Loopy cosy
Upper body

With 4 mm (UK 8, USA 6) circular needles and Orange kid mohair, refer to Method 2, The Holy Cast-On (see page 10) to cast on 8 stitches.

Rnd 1: Knit.
Rnd 2: Increase once in each stitch (by knitting into the front and back of it) to end of round (16 sts).
Rnd 3: *Loop1, K1, repeat from * to end of round.
Rnd 4: *K1, increase once in next stitch, repeat from * to end of round (24 sts).
Rnd 5: *Loop2, K1, repeat from * to end of round.

Rnd 6: *K2, increase once in next stitch, repeat from * to end of round (32 sts).
Rnd 7: *Loop3, K1, repeat from * to end of round.
Rnd 8: *K3, increase once in next stitch, repeat from * to end of round (40 sts).
Rnd 9: *Loop4, K1, repeat from * to end of round.
Rnd 10: *K4, increase once in next stitch, repeat from * to end of round (48 sts).

Continue in this increasing pattern until there are 10 stitches in each segment of the pie (80 sts in total).

OR STOP the increasing pattern earlier, when the circumference of the circle is big enough for the teapot you are using. This might be FEWER than a total of 80 stitches, especially as the loop stitch is very stretchy. Be sure to measure against the teapot with the Lining well before then.

Knit 1 round without shaping.

Sides

Worked in ROWS (not rounds).

Begin working the first Side with the WRONG side facing.

Row 1: Knit to end of row. (Yes, this makes a different stitch to when you were working in the round but you won't be able to see it and it is easier, and it is important to be easy when we can.)
Row 2: Loop to end of row.
Repeat Rows 1 and 2 until the Side measures long enough to cover the bowl of the teapot.

Cast off loosely.

Work the second Side the same.

Putting it all together

Sew the Sides together below the spout and handle using mattress stitch (see page 16).

Place the Loopy Cosy over the Lining and sew the Lining and the outer cosy together around the handle and spout openings.

Froth and Bubble

I bought this little cardie* from a posh department store in Sydney and added the loopy collar and cuffs. After knitting Ranga and Desirée, you will be able to do the loop stitch in your sleep.

*CARDIE: AUSSIE** SLANG FOR CARDIGAN
**AUSSIE: SLANG FOR AUSTRALIAN

MATERIALS

* One posh, ready-made woollen cardie
* 1 x 25 g (⅞ oz) ball Grignasco Knits Kid Seta Mohair 2-ply (lace weight): Colour 462
* Fine cotton, the colour of your cardigan

EQUIPMENT

* One set 2.75 mm (UK 12, USA 2) circular needles, 80 cm (32 in) from tip to tip
* Fine sewing needle
* Scissors

Preparing the cardie

With the cotton double threaded and the fine sewing needle, do blanket stitch (or the hokey-pokey) around the edges of the collar and cuffs, keeping in mind that you will be inserting a 2.75 mm (UK 12, USA 2) needle to make the first row of knit stitches.

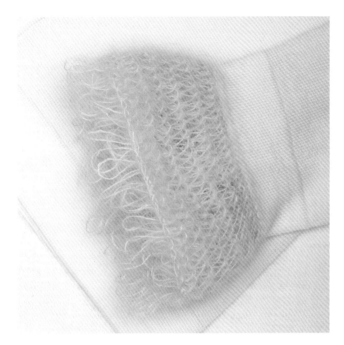

Cuffs

Knitted in the ROUND.

With the wrong side of the cardigan sleeve facing and 2.75 mm (UK 12, USA 2) needles, pick up one kid mohair stitch for each cotton blanket stitch.

Rnd 1: Purl.
Rnd 2: Loop every stitch (see page 14).
Repeat the last 2 rounds 5 more times (12 rows in all).

Cast off loosely.

Collar

Knitted in ROWS.

With the wrong side of the cardigan collar facing and 2.75 mm (UK 12, USA 2) needles, pick up one kid mohair stitch for each cotton blanket stitch.

Note. I worked the left side first, knitting the rows from the middle front left to the centre back only, and then the right side, knitting the rows from centre back to the right front. It was more comfortable to handle than going all the way around at once, that's all.

Row 1: Knit.
Row 2: Loop every stitch (see page 14).
Repeat the last 2 rows 2 more times (6 rows in all).

Cast off loosely.

Finishing off

Time to thread the sewing needle again. The Cuff won't want to fold back naturally, so it will need a little help. Make small tacking stitches with a single cotton thread to secure the Cuff to the sleeve at the very point of the fold.

Pin the Cuff top to the sleeve. The circumference of the knitted Cuff is likely to be bigger than the circumference of the cardie sleeve, so take care to ease the loopy knitted Cuff into place. With needle and single cotton thread, hem into place.

And now of course you will do the same for the Collar.

Bellissimo!

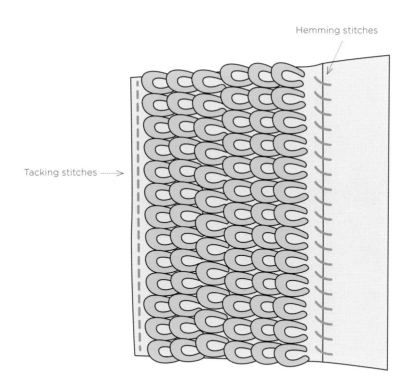

Hemming stitches

Tacking stitches

Graphs

Here are the double knit graphs. If this is your first time, start with the Square of Squares. Trust me! It is invaluable advice.

Heart Throb

Hot Potatoes

Double Knit Neck Warmer
with Woven Windows

Heart Throb

HEART

Heart Throb

HEART

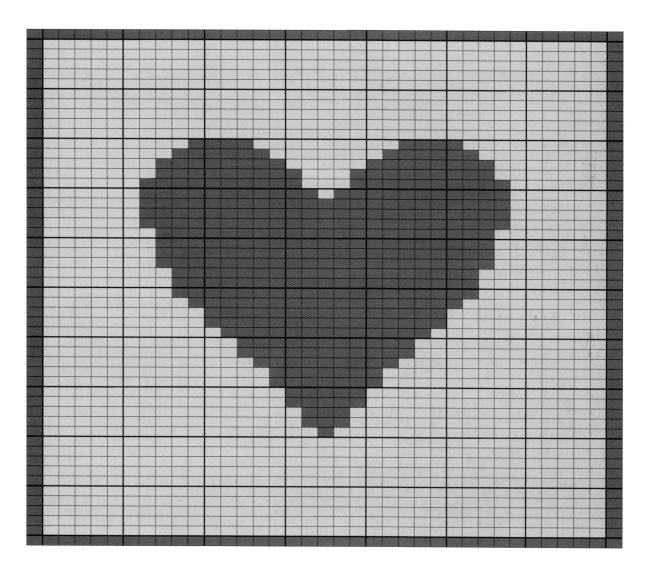

Heart Throb

SQUARE OF SQUARES

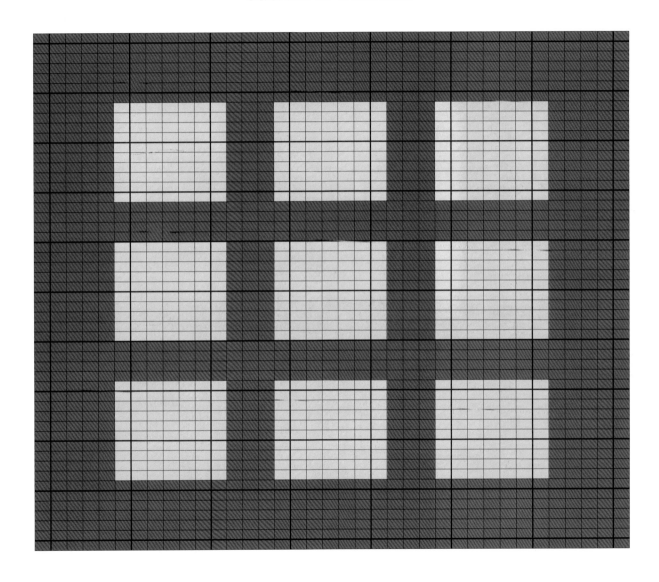

Heart Throb

SQUARE OF SQUARES

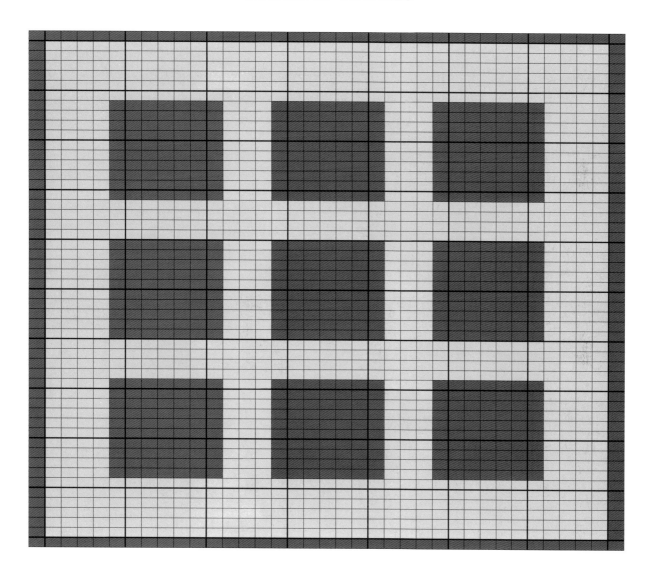

Hot Potatoes

SMALL HEARTS

Pretty Funny Tea Cosies

Hot Potatoes

SMALL HEARTS

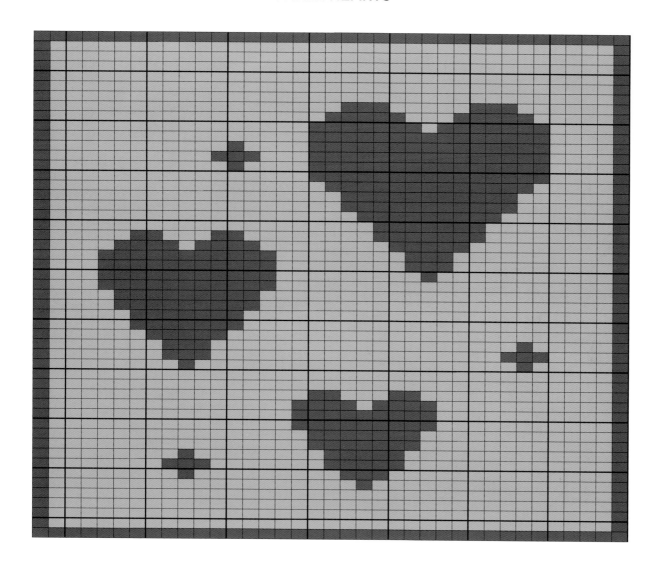

Double Knit Neck Warmer with Woven Windows

BACK: Flat stocking stitch windows facing

On this side, when working the **1st row** of the WINDOWS, *knit* the front stitches and *purl* the back stitches to make a neat colour change. Then each row after that – in the window only – KNIT the front stitches and KNIT the back stitches.

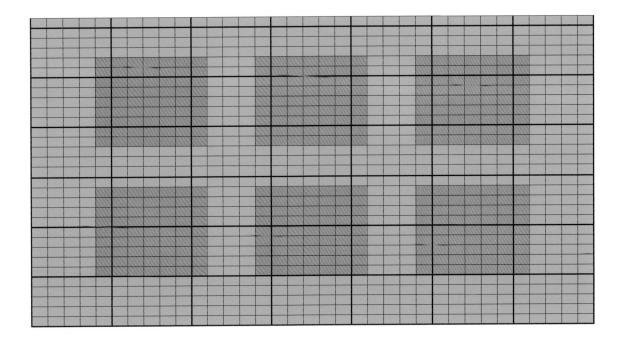

A Very Important Note about working the WINDOWS from the SECOND ROW. When the PURL stitches are facing you, the front fabric yarn will stay at the front always. Only the BACK fabric yarn will move forward and back with each stitch.

Double Knit Neck Warmer with Woven Windows

FRONT: Raised woven windows facing

On this side, when working the **1st row** of the WOVEN WINDOWS, *knit* the front stitches and **purl** the back stitches to make a neat colour change. Then each row after that – in the window only – PURL the front stitches and PURL the back stitches.

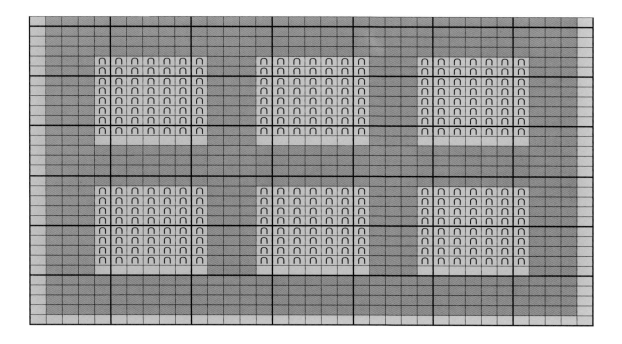

A Very Important Note about working the WINDOWS from the SECOND ROW. When the KNIT stitches are facing you, the back fabric yarn will stay at the back always. Only the FRONT fabric yarn will move forward and back with each stitch.

Abbreviations and terms

Knitting Abbreviations

ABBREV	EXPLANATION
K	knit
P	purl
dpn/s	double-pointed needle/s
st/s	stitch/es
tog	together
cm	centimetre/s
in	inch/es
RS	right side
WS	wrong side
MC	main colour
CC	contrasting colour
garter st	garter stitch (knit every row)
st st	stocking stitch (1 row knit, 1 row purl)
M1	make 1 (see page 15)
ssk	slip slip knit (see page 15)
K2tog	knit two together (see page 15)
increase once in next stitch	knit (or purl, if you are on a purl row) into the front and back of the next stitch.
yfwd	yarn forward (take the yarn over the needle before working the next stitch)

Crochet Abbreviations and Conversions

ABBREV	AUSTRALIA/NZ/UK	ABBREV	US
ch	chain	ch	chain
sl st	slip stitch	slip st	slip stitch
dc	double crochet	sc	single crochet
htr	half treble	hdc	half double crochet

Yarns – Guidelines Only

AUSTRALIA/NZ/UK	US	TENSION/GAUGE
3-ply, 4-ply, 5-ply, jumper weight	fingering	32–26 sts to 10 cm (4 inches)
8-ply, dk, double knit	sport weight – double knit, light worsted	22–24 sts to 10 cm (4 inches)

Stockists

Nundle Woollen Mill
1 Oakenville Street
Nundle NSW Australia 2340
1300 686 353 or +61 (0)2 6769 3330
woollenmill@nundle.com
www.nundle.com

Wool Addiction
Shop 3, 20 Station Street
Bowral NSW Australia 2576
02 4862 4799
info@wooladdiction.com.au
www.wooladdiction.com.au

Tangled Yarns
Studio A/9 Chester Street
Newstead QLD Australia 4006
07 3666 0276
tangled@tangledyarns.com.au
www.tangledyarns.com.au

Mosman Needlecraft
Shop 3, 529 Military Road
Mosman NSW Australia 2088
02 9969 5105
mosmanneedlecraft@bigpond.com
www.mosmanneedlecraft.com.au

Threads and More
Cnr Clarence & Lambert Roads
Indooroopilly QLD Australia 4068
07 3870 1005
shop@threadsandmore.com.au
www.threadsandmore.com.au

Jo Sharp Hand Knitting Yarns
P.O. Box 357
Albany WA Australia 6331
08 9841 4640
info@knit.net.au
www.knit.net.au

Wool Baa
124 Bridport Street
Albert Park VIC Australia 3206
03 9690 6633
sales@woolbaa.com.au
www.woolbaa.com.au

Morris & Sons
50 York St
Sydney NSW Australia 2000
02 9299 8588
sydneystore@morrisandsons.com.au
www.morrisandsons.com.au

Wondoflex Yarn Craft Centre
1353 Malvern Road
Malvern VIC Australia 3144
03 9822 6231
info@wondoflex.com.au
www.wondoflex.com.au

Acknowledgements

You Lot

Ah, this knitty loife. What a surprise. When I sat quietly at home here knitting up *Wild Tea Cosies* all that time ago, I couldn't imagine how my life might be so different with new stuff to learn, new places to visit and the most generous, smart, funny and welcoming new people to play with.

There are You Lot who play with me on-line, the modern pen friends; and You Lot who pay good money to play with me at workshops (that always surprises me), the wonderful workshop women; and You Lot who welcome me into your homes, the hospitable hosts; and You Lot who put up your hands to test knit, the terrific test knitters; and there are You Lot who are ALL of those things.

I like You Lot.

A lot.

Diana Hill – Publisher

For a scary moment there, I thought you'd left me, Diana, but there you were again like an angel to guide me gently, steadily through the ups and downs of publishing. We are bound together forever, parents of three books. Thank you, thank you, thank you.

Mark Crocker – Photographer

Welcome back Mark. First *Wild Tea Cosies* and now *Pretty Funny Tea Cosies*. You are a bloody find, I tell you, a joy to plot and scheme with. A joy to play with. A joy to work with! Thank you for being you.

Lyndel Miller – Stylist

You have the magic Lyndel. My little objets d'art shine in your skilled artfulness.

Georgina Bitcon – Editor

And you too, Georgina. Three books! Nuts. Thank you, thank you, thank you, too.

The Design Team

And just when you thought that was it, there is The Design Team, turning what the rest of us did into something very beautiful, a book. There is the extremely organised and ever diplomatic Editorial Manager, Claire Grady, the very clever and talented Design Manager Miriam Steenhauer and Designer Susanne Geppert. Thank you. Where would we be without you all.

Tea Cosies Excellently Test Knitted by:

Rhonda Kevern
Pamela Lee
Julie Perovic
Sue Averay

Tea Cosies Cleverly Christened by:

Anne Newton
Wendy Ward
And friends

Top Bloke

Oh Jules. Love, love, love.

Published in 2014 by Murdoch Books, an imprint of Allen & Unwin.

Murdoch Books Australia
83 Alexander Street
Crows Nest NSW 2065
Phone: +61 (0) 2 8425 0100
Fax: +61 (0) 2 9906 2218
www.murdochbooks.com.au
info@murdochbooks.com.au

Murdoch Books UK
Erico House, 6th Floor
93–99 Upper Richmond Road
Putney, London SW15 2TG
Phone: +44 (0) 20 8785 5995
www.murdochbooks.co.uk
info@murdochbooks.co.uk

For Corporate Orders & Custom Publishing contact Noel Hammond,
National Business Development Manager, Murdoch Books Australia

Publisher: Diana Hill
Photographer: Mark Crocker
Styling: Lyndel Miller
Designer: Susanne Geppart
Cover Designers: Susanne Geppart and i2i
Design Manager: Miriam Steenhauer
Editor: Georgina Bitcon
Editorial Manager: Claire Grady
Production Manager: Mary Bjelobrk

A cataloguing-in-publication entry is available from the catalogue of the
National Library of Australia at www.nla.gov.au.

A catalogue record for this book is available from the British Library.

Colour reproduction by Splitting Image, Clayton, Victoria.

Printed by 1010 Printing International Limited, China.